FRIENDS
OF ACPL

GRASSHOPPERS
and Their Kin

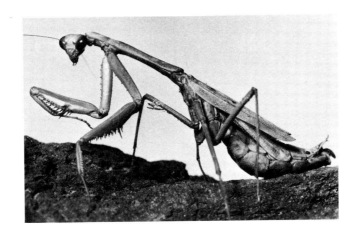

GRASSHOPPERS
and Their Kin

Ross E. Hutchins

Illustrated with photographs by the author

DODD, MEAD & COMPANY · NEW YORK

To Bud and Betty Gaines
for their help in many ways

Frontispiece: A typical long-horned grasshopper *(Orchelimum)* known as a meadow grasshopper. It has very long, slender antennae and is greenish in color. (Life size: 1¼ inches)

ISBN 0-396-06503-1
Library of Congress Catalog Card Number: 70-184186
Printed in the United States of America

ACKNOWLEDGMENTS

The author wishes to thank the following individuals for their aid in furnishing certain pictures and information. These include Dr. E. G. Roberts and Mr. Le Quang Long. Appreciation is due to the Information Service of The Church of Jesus Christ of Latter-day Saints (Mormon Church) for the photograph of the Seagull Monument in Temple Square, Salt Lake City. The author especially appreciates the aid of Dr. Ashley B. Gurney, Specialist in Orthoptera, U. S. National Museum, Washington, D. C., for his help with pictures and for valuable technical information.

CONTENTS

INTRODUCTION

This is the story of those insects classified as Orthoptera, the most important of which are grasshoppers. However, this insect group also includes some related insects whose life histories and habits are unusually interesting. These are the crickets, katydids, mantids, walking-sticks, and cockroaches. It is, indeed, a varied insect assemblage with habits as diverse as their structures and appearances. The grasshoppers are sun-loving and feed upon vegetation; katydids and crickets are most active at dusk; the walking-sticks dwell slothful lives among the leaves of trees and are rarely seen; the cockroaches are creatures of the darkness, feeding upon most anything; the mantids are voracious hunters, capturing and devouring almost any other insect that crosses their paths.

Yet, all these insects, classified in the order Orthoptera, have a common ancestry. They can all trace their lineage back down the eons to the ancient days when the earth was young, to that period more than 300 million years ago when the coal beds were being formed. All these insects, except the cockroaches, have been changed greatly by time and evolutionary processes. Only the lowly roaches still adhere to ancient ways. Progress and change seem to have passed them by; they live now as did their forebears during Carboniferous days, altered but little by the passing millennia.

Since antiquity man has been familiar with grasshoppers that often destroyed his crops, bringing hunger to the land. Their ravages have been noted in the ancient literature of the Egyptians, Hebrews, and Greeks. Regarding grasshopper plagues, it is stated in the Bible, Joel 2:3, that ". . . . the land is a garden of Eden before them, and behind them a desolate wilderness."

9

A typical grasshopper. Like all insects, its body is divided into three sections: head, thorax, and abdomen. The legs and wings are attached to the thorax. This is the lubber grasshopper. (Life size: 3 inches)

CHAPTER 1

THE GRASSHOPPER CLAN

Grasshoppers and crickets are familiar to everyone; they are seen during almost every walk in the country and, even, in city parks. They feed upon vegetation, often harming gardens and crops. Their depredations during ancient times are referred to many times in the Bible, and grasshopper scourges were common in ancient Egypt. Portrayed on a papyrus bloom in the tomb of Haremhab, a Pharaoh of Egypt in the fifteenth century B.C., is an excellent likeness of the destructive desert locust.

It should perhaps be explained at this point that the term "locust" is usually applied to destructive grasshoppers having migratory habits. However, entomologists do not always adhere to this rule and so the terms are more or less interchangeable.

Less familiar to most people are those insects that are closely related to the crickets and grasshoppers. These are the cockroaches, mantids, walking-sticks, and katydids. In fact, it may come as a surprise to some to learn that these latter insects all belong to the grasshopper tribe. Of them all, the cockroaches

11

This portrayal of the destructive desert locust was discovered in the tomb of a Pharaoh of Egypt, fifteenth century B.C. (Reproduced by the author in glass enamel fused onto copper.)

are the most ancient and it was from them that all the others are believed to have descended.

Grasshoppers and their relatives all belong to the insect order Orthoptera. The name Orthoptera is of Greek origin, being derived from two words, *orthos* meaning "straight" and *pteron* meaning "wing." Thus, the name means "straight-winged" and refers to the fact that most of these insects have straight, leathery front wings. This feature is especially evident in the grasshoppers, in which the membranous hind wings are folded fan-like beneath the front wings when the insects are at rest.

A typical grasshopper begins life as an egg buried in the ground. The female bores her abdomen into the soil for perhaps an inch and lays a cluster of from twenty to one hundred eggs. It is in this stage that winter is usually passed. In spring the young grasshoppers hatch and emerge from the ground. At this time they are called *nymphs*. These nymphs look much like their parents except that they are much smaller and have no wings. They begin feeding upon plants and within a few days shed

12

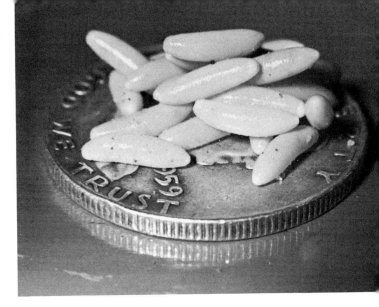

Grasshoppers hatch from eggs laid in the ground, usually in autumn. Shown here are the large eggs of the lubber grasshopper on a fifty-cent piece. (Life size: 1/4 inch)

their skins to allow for increase in size. As weeks pass, the young hoppers or nymphs continue to feed and grow, shedding their skins from five to eight times. After each molt they are slightly larger and wings eventually appear. At the last molt they acquire fully developed wings and are then in the adult stage. Thus, a grasshopper passes through only three main stages in its life history: egg, nymph, and adult. Development is gradual and so they are said to have a *simple* or *gradual* life history or *metamorphosis*. This is in contrast to the *complete* metamorphosis of a moth, butterfly, or beetle which passes through four stages: egg, larva, pupa, and adult. In the case of grasshoppers and their relatives there is no inactive pupal stage.

The grasshopper clan is believed to have descended from very ancient ancestors that lived during, or previous to, the Carboniferous Period, about 300 million years ago. It was during this time that the giant, treelike mosses and ferns flourished and great dinosaurs roamed the earth. The grasshoppers and their kin evolved on the same branch of the insect family tree as the

13

Grasshoppers have gradual life histories. A young hopper is called a nymph and looks much like the adult except for the absence of wings. During its growth it sheds its outer skin several times. This is a typical grasshopper nymph.

termites and earwigs, and their ancestors were cockroach-like. Some were of large size and were very abundant, comprising nearly 60 per cent of the insects that lived at that time. As millions of years passed, the cockroaches declined in abundance while the grasshoppers and crickets increased in number.

The development of wings was an important milestone in the evolution of insects. It seems probable that winged insects came into existence during the Lower Carboniferous. In other words, insects evolved wings at least 50 million years before either reptiles or birds took to the air. Unlike the wings of birds, however, insects' wings were not evolved from legs. By contrast, their wings arose as separate structures. They developed from lateral

This is the nymph of the clouded grasshopper (*Encoptolophus*). At this stage it has short wings.

The adult clouded grasshopper has clear hind wings. It is common in fields. (Life size: 1 inch)

extensions or vanes extending from the sides of their bodies and were probably at first mere gliding organs. Later, muscles to move them were added and powered flight came into existence. This was the evolutionary course followed by the ancestors of the cockroaches, grasshoppers, and related insects. At first all four wings were membranous; later, the front pair became thickened and used to cover the hind pair when at rest.

By the Triassic Period, about 185 million years ago, winged, grasshopper-like insects were in abundance, probably resembling those found today. Fossil wings of these ancient grasshoppers even show that *stridulating* (sound-making) organs were already present. Thus, these insects were probably the first of all animals to have "voices."

In the world there are about 25,000 different kinds or species of grasshoppers and related insects. It is not the largest insect group, since it is far outnumbered in kinds by the beetles (275,000 kinds), the butterflies and moths (112,000 kinds), the two-winged flies (85,000 kinds), and by the wasps, bees, and ants (100,000 kinds). However, if we consider the number of individuals present today we find that grasshoppers are among the most abundant of insects. A walk through a grassy field in summer will convince you of the truth of this statement. At almost every step, grasshoppers will be seen jumping away through the grass. These insects and their relatives are found almost everywhere in the world where climates are warm and plant food available. I have encountered grasshoppers on tiny islands hundreds of miles from other land masses in the vast Pacific Ocean. They looked much like the ones at home, and I wondered how they had become established so far from continental lands.

To primitive people in many parts of the world, grasshoppers often served as food items. Indians of the Southwest ate them

Grasshoppers were eaten by many primitive peoples, including the American Indians. Canned roasted grasshoppers and other insects are available in many novelty food stores.

in large numbers. Along the foothills of the Sierras huge swarms of locusts often congregated in late summer. At such times, entire tribes gathered to collect and roast the insects for winter food. They constituted a source of protein in the Indians' protein-deficient diet. The locusts were eaten whole or ground with *pinole* or acorn meal. In this fashion many tons of locusts were consumed each year. It is of interest, too, that canned grass-hoppers are even now available in novelty food shops, along with such so-called tasty items as rattlesnake meat and preserved caterpillars.

While most people do not regard insects as being choice items of food, grasshoppers were included in a listing of emergency foods in a survival manual issued to our armed services during World War II.

The ancient Greeks considered grasshoppers to be a great delicacy and there are a number of references in both the Old and New Testaments regarding the eating of these common insects. They are often eaten by the Arabs and by people of Oriental lands. Insects of many kinds, including grasshoppers, were, and still are, eaten in many parts of Africa where they are considered to be choice morsels.

17

For one reason or another insects were often emblazoned on coats-of-arms during medieval days. These devices were painted on shields, banners, and the armor of knights and princes. At that time, most people could not read and so these designs were needed as a means of identification. These heraldic decorations were adopted by leaders and were usually family insignia. Often they were very colorful and arrayed with beasts, such as lions or other animals, as well as Latin mottoes. It is of interest here to consider those that portrayed various insects.

Bees were the insects most frequently shown on coats-of-arms. In all, sixty-five families favored these industrious insects. Butterflies were emblazoned on the arms of twenty-one families, beetles on the arms of eleven families, while ants were adopted by nine families. One family crest portrayed a chevron between three hornets; another shows three golden wasps. Strangely, one crest was decorated with fleas!

Grasshoppers were portrayed on the arms of sixteen families and crickets on four. For example, the arms of the Woodward family of Kent shows a black chevron among three green grasshoppers, while the shield of the Crignon family has a chevron with three golden crickets.

Like all insects, grasshoppers and their relatives have *exoskeletons*. That is, their skeletons are on the outside of their bodies. This forms a hard shell within which the body organs, including the muscles, are enclosed and protected. All these insects have chewing mouthparts and feed upon a wide variety of foods. Grasshoppers, walking-sticks, and crickets are mostly plant feeders. Mantids live by capturing and eating other insects. Cockroaches, by contrast, are mostly *omnivorous*, that is, they feed upon both plant and animal foods.

Members of the grasshopper clan that dwell in trees or in the grass are frequently green, a color that probably aids them in

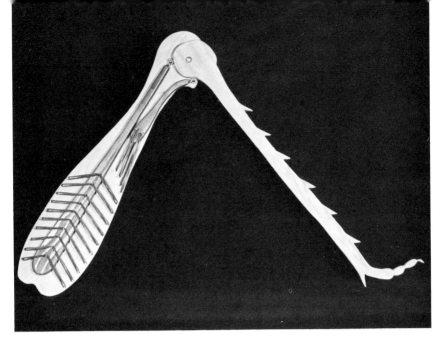

Like all insects, grasshoppers and their kin have "outside" skeletons (exoskeletons) with the muscles inside. This plywood model of a grasshopper's jumping leg is powered by rubber bands (muscles).

escaping the eyes of birds and other enemies. Ground-inhabiting forms are usually of various shades of gray or brown. Most of these insects have well-developed hearing organs; those of the grasshoppers are oval eardrums, or *tympana*, located on each side of the first abdominal segment, while katydids have hearing organs on their front legs. The males of many kinds make sounds by rubbing one body part against another.

Eyes are always present and most members of the grasshopper clan apparently have keen vision, as you soon find if you attempt to capture one of them. Too, the majority are active by day and are sun-loving. However, the katydids and crickets are dusk-loving and it is then that they sing. Cockroaches prefer darkness.

Like most insects, the grasshopper tribe is air-breathing and they do not enter water by choice. However, there are a few kinds that sometimes do take refuge in the water. One of these (*Orchelimum bradleyi*) is found in the Okefenokee Swamp. It is

19

A grasshopper's compound eye is made up of hundreds of individual eyes or facets. This kind of eye is especially adapted to perceiving moving objects.

This photograph was taken through a grasshopper's eye by a special, complicated process. The grasshopper has compound vision.

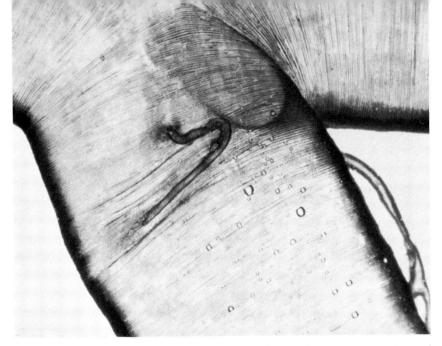

Grasshoppers, like most insects, breathe through spiracles or air vents located along the sides of their bodies. Tiny tubes or tracheae carry air to the internal organs. Shown here is a photomicrograph of one of the branching tracheae in a grasshopper's body.

a long-horned grasshopper and lives among aquatic plants, readily taking to the water when alarmed. It is a good swimmer and usually will cling to the underside of a submerged plant until danger is past. It can remain underwater for several minutes. Even more remarkable is a grasshopper found in Argentina, Uruguay, Peru, and other South American countries. This is a truly aquatic insect. Its scientific name is *Marellia* and its hind legs are shaped like oars, enabling it to swim rapidly. It attaches its eggs to the undersurfaces of water plants such as water lilies. Its normal habitat is upon the leaves of floating plants in ponds and streams.

If you have ever watched a grasshopper at rest you have probably noticed how its abdomen pumps in and out like a bellows. This is because it is forcing air in and out of breathing pores, or *spiracles*, located along the sides of its body. It has been found that as a grasshopper's abdomen expands, air is

21

being sucked in through the front spiracles and when the abdomen is compressed, the air is forced out through the spiracles on the last six abdominal segments. Thus, air is circulated through the tiny tracheal tubes of the body in an efficient manner.

In addition to the typical grasshoppers and locusts, the insect order Orthoptera includes a number of other, closely related insects as follows:

FAMILY TETTIGONIIDAE—
LONG-HORNED GRASSHOPPERS AND KATYDIDS

These insects can usually be recognized by their threadlike antennae which are often longer than their bodies. Their hearing organs (ears), when present, are located on the front legs. Many kinds are bright green in color and the males usually have well-developed sound-making organs located at the bases of the front wings. The females' *ovipositors* (egg-laying tubes) are flattened and their eggs are attached to twigs or inserted in them. Most of them feed on plants. There are many kinds.

FAMILY GRYLLIDAE—CRICKETS

Like most grasshoppers and locusts, these insects have short antennae. Their hearing organs are located on their front legs, while the males' sound-making organs are on the bases of the front wings. The females' ovipositors or egg-tubes are awl-like and eggs are laid either in the ground or inserted in twigs. Some kinds are wingless. Most crickets live on the ground, usually hiding by day under stones or debris. Some, such as the tree crickets, live in trees. There are more than a thousand different kinds.

22

Katydids are closely related to grasshoppers. This green katydid (*Micro-centrum*) dwells in trees and attaches its eggs to twigs. The males have sound-making organs. (Life size: 2 inches)

Crickets are found almost everywhere and sometimes damage crops. Like grass-hoppers, they lay their eggs in the ground. The males have sound-making organs. (Life size: 1 inch)

FAMILY MANTIDAE—PRAYING MANTIDS

These are large, slow-moving insects having their front legs especially fitted for capturing and holding prey consisting, usually, of other insects. These legs are held in front of their bodies as if the insect were in the attitude of prayer. Thus, these insects are commonly called praying mantises or mantids. Technically, they are members of the family Mantidae and so are usually termed mantids by entomologists. Their eggs are laid in masses attached to twigs and hatch in spring. Most mantids are found in tropical countries but several kinds occur in the United States.

FAMILY PHASMATIDAE—WALKING-STICKS

The bodies of these peculiar insects are very elongate, making them resemble twigs. A few tropical kinds have bodies flattened and leaflike. Some are wingless, others have wings. Those found in the United States are wingless. They are slow-moving and feed on the leaves of trees or shrubs. Eggs are dropped upon the ground where they remain until the following spring. They vary in length from an inch or so to more than six inches.

FAMILY BLATTIDAE—COCKROACHES

These are flattened insects with threadlike antennae. Both pairs of wings are of similar texture, usually brown in color. A few kinds are black or marked with color. Eggs are usually laid in capsules containing a number of eggs. Cockroaches vary in size from very tiny to more than three inches long. They feed upon a wide variety of foods, some being pests in homes. There are many kinds, especially in tropical lands.

Above: Praying mantids live on other in-sects which they capture with their spiny front legs. (Life size: 3 inches)

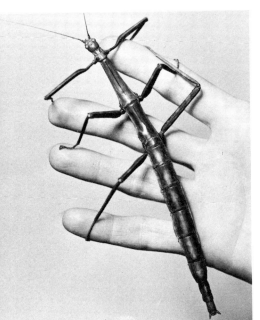

Left: Walking-stick insects mimic twigs and feed on tree leaves. Some kinds have wings. Eggs are dropped to the ground. (Life size: 6 inches)

Below: Cockroaches are ancient insects. Their ancestors were common in Carboni-ferous forests millions of years ago. (Life size: 1 inch)

This close-up shows a lubber grasshopper feeding on a blade of grass.

CHAPTER **2**

GRASSHOPPERS,
MAN'S ANCIENT ENEMY

Of all insects, grasshoppers are probably man's most ancient enemy. In Biblical times swarms of migratory locusts (grass-hoppers) flew over the land, settling down, here and there, to destroy crops. In the book of Exodus it is recorded that ". . . they covered the face of the whole earth, so that the land was darkened; and they did eat every herb of the land, and all the fruit of the trees which the hail had left; and there remained not any green thing in the trees, or in the herbs of the field, through the land of Egypt."

Insects are mentioned in the Bible 120 times. Of these, grasshoppers and locusts are referred to thirty-four times, leaving the reader with the impression that these insects were, indeed, man's most serious and persistant enemy. In Psalms 105:35, it is stated "And [locusts and grasshoppers] did eat up all the herbs in their land, and devoured the fruit of their ground." Today, even as in Biblical times, these pests descend upon fields and orchards in the lands around the Mediterranean, causing tre-

27

mendous damage. The insects involved are the African migratory locusts *(Locusta migratoria)*. These grasshoppers still swarm over these same lands, destroying crops just as they did in former times.

The ravages of these locusts are also described in the literature of ancient Egypt where large numbers of them frequently settled down and fed upon food crops, destroying every green thing. It is of interest that the word "locust" is actually derived from Latin, the original meaning being "a burned place." This gives us a hint as to the appearance of a field after the locusts had finished feeding and flown on.

In America both grasshoppers and locusts have often caused severe damage to rangelands and crops. I once drove across South Dakota shortly after a grasshopper plague. For nearly a hundred miles not a green living plant was to be seen. During an outbreak in Iowa the dead grasshoppers were collected from a measured plot of ground and then weighed. From this it was estimated that on a twenty-acre field there had been 23,250 pounds (eleven and one-half tons) of grasshoppers. This gives us an idea of the tremendous numbers of the insects that may be present during periods of abundance. Locust plagues were especially destructive in the Midwest during the years from 1874 to 1876. As might be expected, these outbreaks caused great economic loss. During this time, for example, the official state constitution of Nebraska had to be rewritten to take care of economic problems arising from loss caused by grasshoppers. As a result, this revised state document became known as "The Grasshopper Constitution."

Probably the most destructive of all American locusts or grasshoppers was the Rocky Mountain grasshopper *(Melanoplus spretus)*. These insects once ravaged the rangelands east of the Rockies in tremendous swarms. It was estimated that one of

Crops are often damaged by grasshoppers. In ancient times fields were devastated by grasshopper hoards. Those shown here are lubber grasshoppers.

This is the lesser migratory locust (*Melanoplus sanguinipes*). It is closely related to the famous Rocky Mountain grasshopper (*M. spretus*) now believed to be extinct. (Life size: 1 inch)

these swarms contained 124 billion individuals and darkened the sky.

The strange thing is that the Rocky Mountain grasshopper is now believed to be extinct, the last living specimen having been found in 1902. Just why it became extinct is a matter of conjecture; it seems probable that the conversion of western rangelands to cultivation changed the ecology to such an extent that the grasshoppers could not survive. However, these insects once were very destructive. It is recorded that in covered-wagon days the immigrants were often forced to halt by swarms of the grasshoppers that destroyed the grass, leaving oxen and horses without food.

The breeding area of these insects was apparently on the eastern slopes of the Rocky Mountains from Canada south to Colorado. During certain years the grasshoppers became unusually abundant and after all the local food had been consumed

30

they began migrating eastward across the prairies. They had long, powerful wings and could fly great distances. However, the Rocky Mountain grasshoppers apparently could not survive for more than a year or two on the prairies and so they disappeared and were not seen again until another mass migration eastward from the slopes of the Rockies occurred.

The Rocky Mountain grasshopper—locust, if you prefer—was closely related to the common red-legged grasshopper (*Melanoplus femur-rubrum*) but had longer, more powerful wings. It was even more closely related to the lesser migratory grasshopper (*Melanoplus sanguinipes mexicanus*) which is also a destructive species. At one time it was believed that the Rocky Mountain grasshopper was merely a variety of the lesser migratory grasshopper. However, Dr. Ashley B. Gurney, the well-known author-

A common grasshopper in the United States is the red-legged grasshopper (*Melanoplus femur-rubrum*). It is related to the migratory locusts that once caused great damage to rangelands in the West.

ity on grasshoppers at the U.S. National Museum, now considers that the extinct Rocky Mountain grasshopper was a distinct species. Whether or not this grasshopper is actually extinct remains to be seen. Dr. Gurney also considers the possibility that the Rocky Mountain grasshopper may have been a long-winged form of the lesser migratory grasshopper that developed, at times, under very special conditions of food or climate.

Whatever the explanation for the former population explosions of Rocky Mountain grasshoppers, they apparently were occurring long before Europeans came to America, perhaps for millions of years. Certainly we have concrete proof of mass flights that took place hundreds of years ago. The evidence of these flights is one of the most amazing of all entomological discoveries.

Located at an elevation of approximately 11,000 feet above sea level in the Beartooth Range of Montana there is a glacier. This glacier is near Yellowstone National Park, north of its northeast corner and is accessible by a trail. It is a region of spectacular grandeur, with some of the surrounding peaks rising to nearly 13,000 feet. In 1940 this glacier was more than a mile in width and nearly that long. During succeeding years there has been a gradual reduction in size due to the melting of the ice. The glacier at its lower end is about 50 feet in thickness and overhangs a small lake. If one looks closely at the face of this glacier it can be seen that there are numerous bands of darker material imbedded in the ice. Upon closer examination it will be found that these dark bands consist, in part, of frozen grasshoppers. This, of course, is the reason that this glacier is known as Grasshopper Glacier and so noted on maps of Montana. Who first discovered these "deep-frozen" insects I have been unable to determine. It is believed, however, that prospectors noticed the insects in the glacial ice in the 1880's. Later, the glacier was

U.S. Department of Agriculture

A glacier in the Beartooth Mountains of Montana at an elevation of 11,000 feet. The face of the glacier is at the left and below it a small lake fed by the melting ice. Millions of grasshoppers (*Melanoplus spretus*) were once trapped in the ice and preserved.

This close-up of the melting face of Grasshopper Glacier in the Beartooth Mountains shows the layers of trapped and frozen grasshoppers. The insects are so well preserved after hundreds of years that fish and birds feed upon them.

U.S. Department of Agriculture

visited by several entomologists. In 1914 some of the grass-hoppers were collected and sent to the U.S. National Museum where they were identified as being specimens of the Rocky Mountain grasshopper.

In any case, there is layer after layer of the insects frozen in the ice, some in an excellent state of preservation. As a matter of fact, they are so well preserved that fish and birds have been seen feeding on them. When visited in 1931, when the glacier was rapidly melting, the odor of great quantities of decaying grasshoppers could be detected a quarter of a mile away. At that time piles of the dead insects had accumulated at the base of the melting glacier to depths of two to four feet.

Naturally, the questions that come to mind are, how did all these grasshoppers become imbedded in the ice and how old are they? The answers to these questions have been puzzling scientists for many years but the chief conclusion is that, in pre-vious years, great, massed flights of Rocky Mountain grasshop-pers were lifted high over the mountains by air currents. Above the glaciers the air was cooled and the flying insects settled upon the ice where they were numbed by the cold and perished. Later, they were covered with falling snow which, in time, froze into ice. Year by year additional flights of grasshoppers were trapped on the surface of the glacier and these too were covered with snow. This accounts for the successive layers of preserved grass-hoppers. In support of the above theory, forest rangers have reported finding living grasshoppers and other insects on the surrounding snow fields each summer. Additional evidence comes from another place in the Rockies. On August 23, 1868, a geological survey party saw large numbers of grasshoppers on snow fields in the valleys near the headwaters of St. Vrain River at the foot of Longs Peak, Colorado. These grasshoppers had been numbed by the cold and were so numerous that they "literally could have been gathered in wagonloads." It was noted that two bears were feeding on them.

As to the age of the grasshoppers preserved in Grasshopper Glacier, specimens subjected to Carbon-14 tests indicate their age as being approximately 600 years This would place the date of their being trapped in the ice about the year A.D. 1350.

The grasshopper glacier in the Beartooth Range of Montana is not the only one where grasshoppers are found imbedded in ice. In central Montana there is another grasshopper glacier located in the Crazy Mountains at the head of Cottonwood Creek and another one a short distance away. African desert locusts have been found frozen in ice on Mount Kilimanjaro and on Mount Kenya, the latter at an elevation of 16,000 feet.

Ranging over most of the eastern United States is the bird locust *(Schistocerca americana)*. This large, long-winged grasshopper measures about three inches in length and is reddish-brown with darker markings. It has powerful wings and often alights in trees when disturbed, no doubt the reason it is known as the bird locust. These common insects are closely related to the desert locust *(S. gregaria)* of Africa and nearby areas. Winter is passed in the adult stage; individuals may often be seen flying over grassy fields on warm days in early spring. They are of little economic importance but one of their relatives, the high plains grasshopper *(Dissosteira longipennis)*, frequently occurs in large numbers in certain western states where it causes tremendous loss to ranchers and farmers. This was especially true during former years before effective insecticides came into use. In several states, including Texas and New Mexico, it was once necessary for the governors to call out the National Guard to aid in spreading poison baits for control of the pests. The most destructive outbreaks occurred between 1936 and 1940. In 1939 it was estimated that 11 million acres of land were infested.

The first authentic report of an outbreak of these locusts was in 1891. That year, these insects, which are not usually common, suddenly increased in abundance in several states. On July 16, 1891, a Denver, Colorado, newspaper *(The Daily News)* published an eyewitness account. The reporter stated that the swarm in eastern Colorado was twenty-three miles wide and seventy miles long. At that time the grasshoppers' wings were not fully developed, but they were hopping eastward at the rate of about four miles a day. It was also stated that the insects clustered on train rails in such numbers as to cause the drive wheels of the locomotives to spin, forcing the trains to stop. This occurred on the Santa Fe Railroad a hundred miles east of Denver. Later, after their wings had developed, the locusts took to the air and flew like birds. The strange thing was that after this mass outbreak the locusts again became relatively rare and damage was only moderate. In 1921, however, they again increased to alarming proportions, especially in eastern Colorado. Since that time there have been several outbreaks of these migratory locusts which remind us of descriptions of the devastations caused by locusts in Biblical times.

While the American grasshoppers and locusts discussed here have often been very destructive, their ravages pale into insignificance by comparison to those wrought by the desert locust *(Schistocerca gregaria)* and the migratory locust *(Locusta migratoria),* both native to the Old World.

The desert locust, slightly over two inches long, ranges across northern Africa to Arabia, Persia, and India. It has powerful wings and can fly long distances, migrating swarms having been encountered by ships in the Atlantic 1,200 miles west of Africa. Swarms of these locusts have appeared in England, the flights probably having originated in southern Algeria, a distance of at least 2,000 miles. The magnitude of one of these migrating

This is the common bird grasshopper (*Schistocerca americana*) of southeastern United States. Its flight is powerful, reminding one of a bird. It is closely related to the desert locust (*S. gregaria*) of the Old World, which may fly for hundreds of miles. (Life size: 2 inches)

swarms is almost unbelievable. In East Africa one such swarm was more than a hundred feet high and a mile in width. The grasshoppers were flying about six miles per hour and took nine hours to pass one point. The strange thing is that the insects usually fly into the wind, especially if it is blowing at less than nine miles per hour.

The migratory locust has an even wider range than the desert locust, being found in Europe, Africa, Asia, Australia, and New Zealand. In appearance these insects look much like the common American bird locust but are slightly smaller in size.

Desert locusts, especially, have been sweeping across Africa and nearby areas for thousands of years and their destructive habits have often caused famine and suffering. In the past, thousands of people have died.

Scientists have been puzzled for a long while as to just what causes the sudden increases in locust populations at certain times. This same characteristic applies to the Old World locusts as well as to those in America. This question now seems to have been settled as a result of research carried out by Sir Boris Uvarov of the Anti-Locust Research Centre in London and by scientists in the United States. In London the research dealt with the desert locust but other migratory locusts probably have similar habits.

In the arid regions of Africa rainfall is usually deficient, with the result that locust populations remain low. Individual hoppers, during such times, live as scattered, solitary insects. Their color is green. When wet years occur, however, vegetation flourishes and food becomes abundant. The locusts begin increasing in numbers. A typical example was 1967 when rains came, creating conditions favorable to locust reproduction. The outcome was a locust population explosion. Suddenly, as a result of crowding, the new generation of locusts not only changed color but also its habits. Whereas they had previously been green in color, they were now marked with black, yellow, and red. Too, instead of being solitary they took on gregarious habits. All this, it has been found, results from hormones or chemical regulators produced by the males. The large numbers of eggs that were laid in 1967 produced fantastic numbers of locusts that swarmed across Africa in 1968. It is thus evident that these locusts have Dr. Jekyll-Mr. Hyde characteristics, the change from the harmless variety into the destructive form being triggered by a favorable season followed by a dry, unfavorable one. During the unfavorable season the locusts are forced to crowd together upon the small amount of available food. This crowding exposes the females to the males' hormones and reproduction is stimulated. The large number of locusts that result must find food and so they swarm across the land, devouring whatever plants are available.

In Mexico and lands to the south, locusts often cause considerable destruction. Many years ago the Mexican government sought to raise funds for the battle against these pests by issuing a special one-centavo stamp that was required to be placed on all letters in addition to the regular postage. However, the project was a failure since additional locusts flew in from Guatemala and countries farther south. Like so many insect-eradication programs, that of eliminating the locusts was doomed to failure. Insects are not easily eradicated.

Thus do man's ancient enemies, the locusts, periodically increase to epidemic proportions and destroy his crops and grasslands. It is a story as old as man himself.

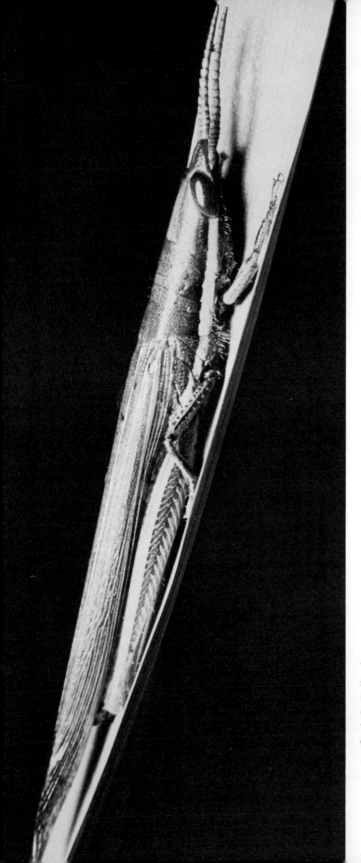

This strange grasshopper is the slant-faced marsh hopper (*Leptysma*). Its form and coloration make it difficult to see when it is resting on a blade of grass. (Life size: 1 inch)

CHAPTER 3

HABITS OF HOPPERS

The life histories of the various kinds of short-horned grass-hoppers are all rather similar. Most kinds lay their eggs in the ground and their young feed upon plants. To most people, one grasshopper looks much like another, yet there are certain differences in their habits and structures and each kind has its own special characteristics.

FAMILY TETRIGIDAE—THE PYGMY OR GROUSE LOCUSTS

To this small family belong the smallest of the short-horned grasshoppers. They are not well known and, because of their diminutive size and secretive habits, are seldom seen. They are easily distinguished from other grasshoppers by the fact that their *pronotum* (the covering of the thorax) extends back beyond the tip of the abdomen. In other short-horned grasshoppers the pronotum fits over the back like a saddle and is not extended toward the rear. Their front wings are much reduced in size,

41

Grouse locusts are small grasshoppers that live in meadows or along the margins of streams. This one (*Neotettix*) was found at the edge of a pond. (Life size: 1/2 inch)

or absent, and they are poor flyers. However, specimens have have been trapped 2,000 feet above ground. Their hind legs are fitted for jumping. These active little insects have no sound-making organs and probably no hearing organs.

Grouse locusts are usually found near the margins of ponds and streams and, when pursued, do not hesitate to take to the water where they are able to dive or swim. Usually they are colored to match the places where they live, a fact that makes them difficult to see. Winter is spent in hibernation in the adult stage and they lay their eggs in spring. Their food habits are unusual for grasshoppers; they feed upon fungi, algae, mosses, lichens, grasses, seeds, and other plant materials, but none is of economic importance.

In the world there are about 650 different kinds of grouse or pygmy locusts, most of which live in the tropics. About 200 kinds occur in North and South America.

FAMILY ACRIDIDAE—TYPICAL SHORT-HORNED GRASSHOPPERS

This large family includes most of the typical grasshoppers seen in fields and roadsides. The males sing during the day, either by rubbing the inner surfaces of the hind legs against the edges of the front wings or by rubbing the front and hind wings together. Many kinds are destructive. This family is divided into three subfamilies as follows:

SUBFAMILY LOCUSTINAE—THE SPUR-THROATED GRASSHOPPERS

These grasshoppers are characterized by having a tubercle or short spine between the front legs. This structure is easily seen. To this large group belong most of our destructive grasshoppers and locusts, including the American or bird locust (*Schistocerca*) and the large lubber grasshoppers, as well as the Old World locusts described in ancient writings.

While most of these grasshoppers have faces that are nearly verticle in profile, there are a few whose faces slant backward from the top. One of these is the slant-faced marsh grasshopper (*Leptysma*) often seen clinging to grasses in marshy areas in the Southeast. Its body is very slender and streamlined, making it difficult to see as it rests quietly on a blade of grass. These grasshoppers should not be confused with the true slant-faced grasshoppers belonging to another subfamily.

Among the most common, and often destructive, of the spur-throated grasshoppers are those classified in the genus *Melanoplus*. To this large group belong the famous Rocky Mountain grasshopper (*M. spretus*), the two-striped grasshopper (*M. bivittatus*), the differential grasshopper (*M. differentialis*), the

Spur-throated grasshoppers have a short spine on the throat. This one, the large bird locust (*Schistocerca americana*), is common in the Southeast. (Life size: 3 inches)

lesser migratory grasshopper *(M. sanguinipes)*, and the common red-legged grasshopper *(M. femur-rubrum)*.

The two-striped grasshopper may be identified by two conspicuous light-colored stripes running down its back. It general color is greenish-yellow with contrasting black or brown markings. It is about one and one-fourth inches long.

The common differential grasshopper is slightly larger, measuring nearly one and one-half inches long and is mottled with contrasting black markings. The thighs of its jumping legs have a series of black chevrons. These grasshoppers often damage gardens and field crops, especially in the southern states.

Common in most parts of the country is the little red-legged grasshopper, measuring hardly three-fourths of an inch long. It is reddish-brown above the yellowish underparts. Its hind legs are bright red.

The lesser migratory grasshopper is somewhat larger than the preceding, measuring about an inch in length. It is reddish-brown with an irregular black patch on its neck or collar. Its habits are more migratory than any of our common grasshoppers. They are strong flyers, often gathering in swarms which fly hundreds of miles. Wherever they stop they destroy crops or range plants. Damage by these grasshoppers has often occurred in the Midwestern states and in Canada. They are close relatives of the Rocky Mountain grasshoppers, now believed to be extinct.

The lubber grasshoppers, largest of all North American species, also belong to this subfamily. These large, heavy-bodied insects occur across the southern portions of the United States. There are several kinds: *Romalea microptera* is found in the Southeast, while *Brachystola magna* is native to the Southwest. The latter species ranges as far north as Kansas.

This is a nymphal spur-throated grasshopper (*Melanoplus*). At this stage its wings are very short. (Life size: 1/2 inch)

These clumsy insects are black with orange-red markings and have short wings that are useless for flight. However, when disturbed they may flutter their wings as if attempting to fly. They often invade gardens where they damage plants by their voracious appetites. They crawl about on the ground or on plants, moving slowly, their large eyes giving them the appearance of intelligence. Actually, they are stupid insects with awkward habits. When picked up in the fingers they make hissing sounds by forcing air from spiracles or air holes in the sides of their bodies. Sometimes a brownish froth is emitted from the spiracles on the thorax. Probably this substance is repellent to certain enemies, especially to ants.

These large hoppers are very cooperative photographic subjects. When placed before a camera and given a blade of grass, a lubber grasshopper begins munching at once in a most nonchalant manner, totally oblivious of the lens.

As in most grasshoppers, eggs are laid in the ground, often as many as eighty, and these hatch in spring. The young hoppers remain together in little groups, hopping or walking slowly about, sometimes climbing up on plants to feed. Later, they separate, each one going its own way. They probably have enemies, but birds are not fond of them, due probably to their disagreeable taste.

Deep in the Everglades of Florida I have often encountered these sluggish grasshoppers walking about as if on some important mission. My most interesting experience with them, however, was the discovery of their breeding areas on an uninhabited island in the vast Pascagoula Swamp along the Gulf Coast. It was autumn and I had visited the island by houseboat. While exploring the terrain I came upon several sandy patches, perhaps six feet in diameter. I was astonished at seeing large numbers of lubber grasshoppers congregated on these bare

This lubber grasshopper was discovered in the act of laying its eggs in the ground on an island near the Gulf Coast. Its abdomen is inserted in the sand. (Life size: 3 inches). (See next photograph)

areas and, on further observation, discovered that they were mating and laying their eggs in the sand. Wishing to obtain photographs of their egg-laying activities, I located a female with her abdomen buried in the soil and carefully scraped away the sand so that her abdomen was completely exposed and the eggs could be seen as they issued from her body. Meanwhile, she continued to lay her eggs, completely oblivious of my presence, while I set up my camera and began taking pictures.

In studying these sandy patches on the island I also found

So intent was the grasshopper that she continued laying eggs when the sandy soil was scraped away. Her eggs are covered with a foam that later hardens into a protective covering.

In autumn lubber grasshoppers apparently congregate on this sandy spot on the Gulf Coast island to mate, lay their eggs, and die. Note several dead grasshoppers and two live ones.

many dead grasshoppers. Seemingly, the insects gather at these locations in autumn to mate, to lay their eggs and then to die. I was reminded of the fable of the graveyard of the elephants, where old elephants are supposed to congregate and die. At summer's end the lubber grasshoppers' eggs are safely hidden in the ground and so, in Nature's scheme, the adults' function in life is finished and they die.

SUBFAMILY OEDIPONINAE—THE BAND-WINGED GRASSHOPPERS

Members of this group have rounded heads in most cases, and their hind wings are yellow or red, banded with black. They are quite conspicuous in flight because of their bright colors, and they usually make crackling sounds with their wings. There are many different kinds, some of which are destructive. One is the Carolina locust (*Dissosteira carolina*), a large insect with black hind wings having yellow margins. The destructive high plains grasshopper (*D. longipennis*) also belongs to this group. Another

49

is the red-winged locust *(Paradolophora)* whose hind wings are red with black borders. One of the important pest species is the clear-winged grasshopper *(Camnula pellucida)* which, as the name indicates, has clear, unmarked hind wings.

SUBFAMILY ACRIDINAE—THE SLANT-FACED GRASSHOPPERS

These grasshoppers can usually be distinguished by the shape of the head. When seen in profile the "face" slants backward from the top of the head. This is true of most members of the subfamily, but there are exceptions. These grasshoppers are usually found in grassy meadows or roadsides and many kinds are green in color. A common example is the green slant-faced grasshopper *(Tryxalis)* whose females may be either green or brown and considerably larger than the males. Another is the striped slant-face *(Mermiria)*, a green grasshopper having a dark stripe down each side. It has flattened antennae.

GRASSHOPPER ENEMIES

Grasshoppers have many enemies, including other insects as well as mammals and birds. Mantids, close relatives of grass-hoppers, capture and feed upon them. There are certain flies (family Nemestrinidae) whose larvae live as parasites in the bodies of grasshoppers. These flies are usually quite rare but in eastern Montana were found to be quite abundant. The females lay large numbers of eggs in cracks in fence posts. When these eggs hatch the tiny larvae are scattered by winds, and when one of them finds a grasshopper it bores into its abdomen where it lives as a parasite. Eventually the grasshopper is killed. In one case 80 per cent of one kind of range grasshoppers was para-sitized by these flies. In addition to these, there are flies belong-ing to the families Tachinidae and Sarcophagidae whose larvae

50

In the fall the Carolina locust (*Dissosteira carolina*), a band-wing, bores its abdomen into the ground to deposit its masses of eggs. This one was photographed in the Great Smoky Mountains. (Life size: 2 1/2 inches)

There are many kinds of slant-faced grasshoppers. This nymphal specimen was photographed in early summer. Later it will develop wings. (Life size: 1/3 inch)

are also parasitic in the bodies of grasshoppers as well as in other insects.

There are several digger wasps that capture grasshoppers. After paralyzing them with their stings, the grasshoppers are carried into underground tunnels where they serve as food for the wasps' young. One of these is the great golden digger wasp (*Sphex ichneumonaeus*) that often captures grasshoppers larger than itself but is able to fly with them to the tunnel it has previously excavated in the ground. Having deposited the inactive grasshopper in her tunnel, the wasp then lays an egg on it and closes the tunnel entrance with earth or sand. Meanwhile, the wasp egg hatches and the larva begins feeding upon the luckless hopper, eventually killing it. In time, the larva becomes full grown and changes into an adult wasp. Sphex wasps of many other kinds also prey upon short-horned grasshoppers or their relatives, the long-horned grasshoppers and crickets.

Robber flies (family Asilidae) also capture grasshoppers, especially young individuals. In this case, however, the hoppers serve as food for their captors instead of their young.

Most unusual are the habits of blister beetle larvae (family Meloidae) that feed upon the underground egg-masses of grasshoppers. There are many kinds of blister beetles, some of which are garden pests. The larvae of these beetles, however, have very unusual life histories. They pass through several distinct stages during their development. This is called a *hypermetamorphosis*. During the first stage the larva has long legs and is very active. It is called a *triungulin* and seeks out a mass of grasshopper eggs and begins feeding on them. At the next stage, the larva's legs are shorter, and later it becomes grublike and has no legs. Later still, having devoured all the grasshopper eggs, it changes into a pupa and then into an adult blister beetle. Often these beetles are very abundant and no doubt destroy many grasshopper egg-masses.

52

Sphex wasps capture and paralyze grasshoppers and place them in their underground burrows as food for their young. This is the golden sphex (*Sphex ichneumoneus*). (Life size: 1 inch)

Here a sphex wasp drags a green cricket toward her underground burrow. These wasps also prey upon grasshoppers. (Life size: 1 inch)

Grasshoppers have many enemies. Robber flies often capture and eat young grasshoppers. (Life size: 1/2 inch)

Grasshoppers also fall victims to a number of parasitic worms that live inside their bodies, eventually killing them.

Birds of many kinds find grasshoppers choice items of diet. One of these is the little sparrow hawk. A stomach of one of these birds contained many black crickets, while another was filled with grasshoppers.

Mammals, too, often devour grasshoppers. In the Southeast, where armadillos are common, they often eat many grasshoppers along with numerous other insects. In the West, the spotted ground squirrel frequently consumes large numbers of grasshoppers, even though it is usually considered to be a vegetarian. The spotted skunk of Arizona sometimes feeds exclusively on grasshoppers. Skunks, of course, in other places, also eat grasshoppers, insects constituting a large part of their diets.

One of the more unusual of the grasshopper eaters is the

Grasshoppers have many internal parasites. This nematode or hair worm emerged from this lubber grasshopper nymph after developing inside its body. The grasshopper died as a result.

grasshopper mouse *(Onychomys)* of the West. These attractive mice are also known as "scorpion mice" because they frequently eat these creatures. Another name for them is "calling mice" because they sometimes utter shrill whistling sounds at dusk or at night on the sagebrush plains. These interesting little mice usually feed upon grasshoppers, crickets, scorpions, beetles, caterpillars, and other insects.

It might, perhaps, seem unusual that gray foxes sometimes eat grasshoppers, yet this is often the case. I once had an experience that proves this. I had acquired two very young foxes in the hopes of obtaining photographs of them. Somehow they escaped from the cage in my backyard and I assumed that they had returned to their native haunts. A month later, at dusk, I saw them at the far side of the lot, jumping after grasshoppers. They had grown considerably larger and had denned under a pile of logs. These little foxes remained in the backyard all summer, emerging each evening at dusk to feed. They were, of course, amusing "pets" and interesting to watch. However, when autumn came, one of my neighbors reported that "something" had been invading his chicken house and capturing his prize pullets; my foxes had evidently graduated to larger game. They had to go.

This is the true katydid (*Ptero-phylla camellifolia*). The males sing very loudly but are not often seen, since they live high in forest trees. (Life size: 1 1/2 inches)

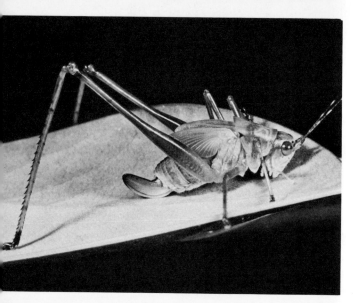

This false katydid (*Ambly-corypha*) lives in trees as do most katydids. This is an immature specimen. (Life size: 1 inch)

This is a nymphal cone-headed katydid (*Neoconocephalus*). Note its swordlike ovipositor. (Life size: 1 inch)

CHAPTER **4**

THE LONG-HORNED
GRASSHOPPERS AND KATYDIDS

It is not unusual, on rambles through fields and forests, to see green grasshoppers, sometimes of large size, their bodies often measuring more than three inches in length. These are long-horned grasshoppers characterized by very long antennae and, usually, green coloration. Some kinds are called katydids because of the calls of the males. There are several thousand different kinds.

While most long-horned grasshoppers are winged and green in color, there are a number that are wingless and live upon the ground, resembling crickets more than grasshoppers, and so are usually called crickets. An example is the Mormon cricket of western United States.

Tree-inhabiting kinds, usually known as katydids, are almost always green, probably an adaptation for protective coloration among the leaves where they live. All these insects belong to the family Tettigoniidae.

THE KATYDIDS

These are medium to large, grasshopper-like insects, green in color, usually found in trees or shrubs. Their antennae are very slender, often longer than their bodies. The ovipositors of the females are either swordlike or sickle-like. As in the case of typical grasshoppers, their hind legs are large and fitted for jumping. Most kinds feed upon vegetation and usually remain resting quietly among leaves during the daylight hours. The males sing at dusk or during the early part of the night. Their songs or sounds are made by rubbing a file on the base of the left front wing against a scraper on the base of the opposite wing. In a few cases, the females, too, have these stridulating organs, but the sounds they make are much more subdued than those made by the males. Some katydids attach their disc-shaped eggs to twigs, while others insert their eggs in the edges of leaves. When confined in a cage, the females have been known to make slits in the edges of ordinary paper in which they inserted their eggs. It is in the egg stage that winter is usually passed in cool climates.

Among the better known katydids is the green, leaflike katydid *(Pterophylla camellifolia)* of eastern United States. Its front wings resemble leaves complete with veins and its body measures more than an inch in length. It sings at dusk. Another kind is the narrow-winged katydid *(Scudderia furcata)*, ranging over most of the United States. It sings during the day or early evening.

Common in most localities is the cone-headed katydid *(Neoconocephalus)* whose head is cone-shaped and extends forward beyond the bases of its antennae. Often seen in grassy areas is the large meadow grasshopper *(Orchelimum)*. There are many kinds.

58

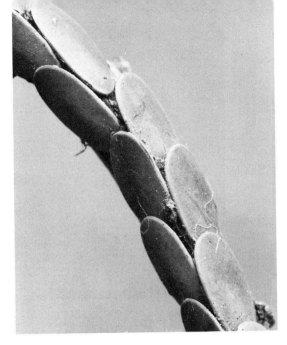

Katydids attach their disc-shaped eggs to the twigs of trees.

Right: With this bladelike ovipositor the false katydid inserts its eggs in leaves.

Below: This strange little creature is a katydid recently hatched from the egg. (Life size: 1/4 inch)

The angular-winged katydid (*Microcentrum*) lives in trees. Its wings are green and resemble leaves. The males have efficient singing organs. This one was photographed in a hemlock in the Great Smoky Mountains. (Life size: 2 inches)

A head-on view of the previous specimen shows the katydid's ears located on its "elbows."

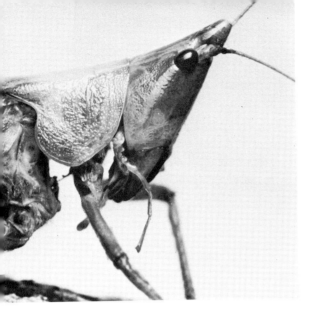

Above: Profile of cone-headed katydid (*Neoconocephalus*). Right: "Portrait" of another cone-headed katydid (*Pyrocorypha*).

Below: "Portrait" of a meadow grasshopper (*Orchelimum*). Right below: "Portrait" of cone-headed katydid (*Neoconocephalus*).

This long-horned grasshopper (*Camptonotus carolinensis*) has no wings. It is known as the leaf-rolling cricket. During the night it emerges from hiding and feeds upon plant lice or aphids. (Life size: 1 inch). (See next photographs)

THE LEAF-ROLLING CRICKET

These cricket-like insects are among the most unusual of the grasshopper tribe. Leaf-rolling crickets *(Camptonotus carolinensis)* are wingless, about two inches in length, and with extremely long antennae. As might, perhaps, be guessed from their long antennae, they are night-active, or nocturnal, in habits. They are peculiar in several respects: at night they emerge from hiding and hunt for plant lice or aphids, upon which they feed; before dawn they find suitable leaves and build shelters in which they remain during the hours of daylight.

After a night of feeding upon aphids a leaf-rolling cricket locates a leaf and makes several slits in it, using its jaws to cut the blade. The insect then places its body between the slits and pulls the severed section around itself, using its feet for the purpose. When the edges of the leaf approach each other, the cricket begins secreting strands of silk from its mouth, moving its head back and forth from one edge to the other. In this way

62

Just before dawn the leaf-rolling cricket cuts a section from a leaf and rolls it around itself. It uses silk to hold its leaf shelter together.

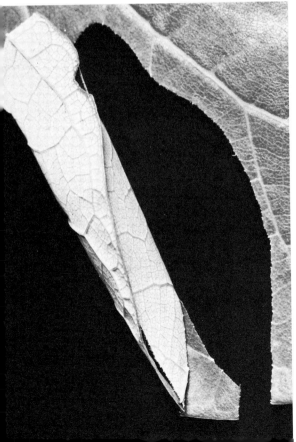

The completed shelter. The leaf-rolling cricket remains in this shelter all day. A new one is built each night.

the edges of the leaf are slowly pulled together, forming a tube-like shelter or tent. There is considerable variation in the construction of this tent; sometimes the cricket finds it necessary to emerge from the tent during its construction in order to fasten the edges. In any case, the tent is eventually finished and the cricket crawls inside, curls its long antennae about itself, and settles down for the day. It builds a new shelter each night. Safe in its green tent the cricket is relatively protected from birds and most other enemies.

The use of silk by a grasshopper or cricket is most unusual, as is the habit of feeding upon aphids. Too, the ability to "build" anything is rarely found among the orthoptera. I once had several of these crickets in captivity in a cage built of sheet plastic. I sat up most of several nights observing how they built their shelters and was surprised at seeing them cut slits in the plastic and form it into shelters just as they do with leaves.

The discovery of the peculiar habits of these crickets followed the usual pattern; entomologists collected specimens and placed them in a museum, knowing nothing about their habits. A technical description of the insect was published in a German scientific journal more than a hundred years ago. Many years later a cricket was discovered rolled up in a pawpaw leaf in the vicinity of Washington, D.C. When the insect was collected and identified it was found to be the same kind of cricket described in the German journal. These remarkable crickets are now known to be rather common in many places in eastern United States.

THE MORMON CRICKET

Mormon crickets (*Anabrus simplex*) are wingless insects of cricket-like form found in Utah and nearby areas of the Rocky Mountains. They are of pale or greenish coloration and nearly

64

U.S. Department of Agriculture
This is the famous Mormon cricket (*Anabrus simplex*), a long-horned grasshopper that often devastates rangelands and crops in the West. (Life size: 1 1/2 inches)

two inches in length. They are heavy-bodied and just back of the head is a saddle-like shield (the pronotum), the reason that these insects are sometimes called "shield-backed grass-hoppers." The female has a long, swordlike ovipositor attached to the tip of her abdomen and she lays her eggs in autumn, depositing them in holes in the bare ground. She may lay as many as a hundred eggs.

These are day-active insects, resting quietly at night, usually on low vegetation. The males utter their rasping songs during the morning up until about ten o'clock. These strange insects are voracious feeders; they devour almost any type of vegetation from sagebrush to cultivated crops. They are also cannibalistic to a marked degree and have the habit of attacking weaker or injured individuals and devouring them. As might be expected from the nature of their food habits, they often cause great damage to crops.

When the Mormons came to the Salt Lake Valley in 1848 and began planting crops they soon discovered that these

U.S. Department of Agriculture

In the vicinity of Salt Lake City, seagulls often feed upon the hoards of migrating crickets.

crickets were serious enemies and that all their agricultural efforts had been in vain. They had no insecticides to protect their crops and were actually faced with starvation. At this dark hour, much to the Mormons' elation, they saw large numbers of seagulls gathering and gorging themselves upon the heavy-bodied crickets. Orson F. Whitney in his *History of Utah*, published in 1892, states that "They [the Mormons] were saved, they believed, by a miracle . . . Just in the midst of the work of destruction great flocks of gulls appeared, filling the air with their white wings and plaintive cries, and settled down on the half-ruined fields . . . all day long they gorged themselves, and when full, disgorged and feasted again . . . until the pests were vanquished and the people were saved. The heaven-sent birds then returned to the lake islands whence they came."

To the Mormons it appeared as if Providence had sent the gulls to save their crops and so a statue was eventually erected in Salt Lake City portraying the seagulls as saviors of the early Mormon settlement.

Mormon crickets often become very abundant in the late summer, at which time they travel in large bands, all moving in the same direction. They travel as much as a mile a day and may migrate as far as fifty miles before beginning to lay eggs.

Right: In Temple Square, Salt Lake City, the Mormons erected this statue to the seagulls which are credited with saving the crops of the first Mormon settlers in Salt Lake Valley. *The Mormon Church, Salt Lake City, Utah*

Lettering on Seagull Statue in Temple Square, Salt Lake City, Utah. *The Mormon Church, Salt Lake City, Utah*

They walk slowly along, often crossing highways and roads in large numbers. I have seen places where the highway was very slippery from the crushed bodies of these insects. The dead individuals were being fed upon by their living companions.

The food habits and preferences of these peculiar insects are very unpredictable; a band of them may march through one field without causing damage and then destroy the next field. When on the march they "eat like horses." It was once estimated that a cricket population of ten per square yard would, during their lives, consume 120 tons of forage (dry weight) per section of land (640 acres). This amount of forage would pasture forty-four head of cattle for nine months.

During the early days in the West, a wide variety of methods were tried for the control of these pests. Ditches were dug around grain fields and these were filled with running water. However, since many of the crickets could climb out of the ditches, various methods of killing them were experimented with. One of the most effective was that of covering the surface of the water with kerosene. Less effective, but quite ingenious, was a set of rollers extending across the ditch or canal at water level. These rollers were rotated by a water wheel, crushing the crickets that floated against them. This method was tried in Idaho in 1905.

In other cases, the cricket hoards were beaten back with brooms and sticks. In most instances these efforts were of little avail; as fast as the front ranks of marching crickets were killed, millions more took their places. A very effective method of control consisted of surrounding the fields with foot-high board barriers topped by metal strips. These barriers stopped the advance of the migrating crickets but, since the crickets accumulated in tremendous numbers in front of the fences, it was necessary to dig pits at intervals into which they would fall. In other

Mormon crickets are sometimes so abundant as to make highways slippery where they are crossing in large numbers.

U.S. Department of Agriculture

Metal barriers, right, are often used to prevent the spread of wingless Mormon crickets in the West. The crickets are seen congregating on the vegetation and on fence posts.

cases pens were constructed where the insects would congregate and be killed.

All of the above methods of combating Mormon crickets were employed before effective insecticides came into use.

In the West there are several other shield-backed crickets that often become very abundant and destructive. One of these is the coulee cricket (*Pernabrus scabricollis*) of the Northwest. To the early settlers, however, one kind looked much like another and they were not interested in technical details of insect classification. At various times and places they were called western crickets, buffalo crickets, mountain crickets, Utah crickets, Idaho crickets, and Great Plains crickets.

Francis Parkman, in *The Oregon Trail* (1872), states that he saw insects in the mountains north of the present city of Laramie, Wyoming, in 1846 that were without doubt Mormon crickets. He, in company with a group of Indians, advanced up a stream in search of buffalo. At one point a council was held to determine the location of the herd. Old Chief Mene-Sella sat down with the other chiefs and picked up an enormous cricket known to the Dahcotah Indians by a name that signified "they who point to the buffalo." Presumably, the cricket told him where to find the herd.

Before the coming of the white man, Mormon crickets were eaten in large numbers by western Indians. While these ungainly insects may be repulsive to us as food items, early trappers found the soup made of them by the Indians to be good and extremely rich. More often the crickets were gathered in the fall and dried or roasted and then pounded into coarse meal as winter food. It is also recorded that the dried crickets were ground in stone grinders with grass seeds and then baked.

This is the strange Jerusalem or sand cricket of the West. These large-headed insects live under stones, in caves, holes in the ground, or similar places. They feed upon both animal and vegetable material. (Life size: 1 inch)

CHAPTER 5

CRICKETS AND
THEIR RELATIVES

Crickets have been known to man for thousands of years. In old England the song of the cricket was a symbol of peace, contentment, and good luck, as is indicated by Charles Dickens' *The Cricket on the Hearth*. The French entomologist, Jean Henri Fabre, says of them, "I know of no insect voice more gracious, more limpid in the profound peace of the nights of August." On the other hand, Hal Borland, a nature writer, wrote in *The New York Times* that ". . . it has six legs, which make it an insect; two antennae, which make it a creature of sensitive feelings; two wings that can be scraped together, which make it a nuisance."

To our ears the male cricket's song may resemble a series of discordant clicks, but to the female it is evidently an attractive love song. However, it is believed by some that the male's song may be a warning to other males to stay out of his territory and thus not a love song at all.

The word "cricket" was derived from the sound made by the

male insect and so it is an onomatopoetic word—a word that sounds like the thing it describes. Thus, to some human ears the common black cricket sounds as if it were saying, "Cree-ket, cree-ket," and so the insect is called a cricket. In France the word for cricket is *criquet*, meaning also to rattle or creak, again the word imitating the sound it makes. The Cherokee Indians were more interested in these insects' habits of gnawing hair from furs. To them they were known as *talatu*, meaning "barber" or "hair-cutter."

Properly speaking, the term cricket should be applied only to members of the insect family Gryllidae. However, several other orthopterous insects are also called crickets and so will be included in this chapter.

THE BLACK CRICKETS—FAMILY GRYLLIDAE

To this family belong some of the best-known insects. Most common are the black or field crickets, *Acheta (Gryllus) assimilis,* found in almost all parts of the United States. Other species occur in other areas of the world, and every country has its black crickets of one kind or another. The species eulogized in *The Cricket on the Hearth* was *Gryllus domesticus.* The common black cricket of China is *Gryllus chinensis.* In Sicily and North Africa there occurs the shrill house cricket (*Brachytrypes megacephalus*) whose call may be heard for nearly a mile.

Black crickets are approximately an inch long and black in color. The female has a slender egg-laying tube, or ovipositor attached to her abdomen and she lays her eggs in the soil. Usually these crickets hide under stones or old boards during the day and the males give their serenades at dusk or early night. These common insects normally feed upon plants or plant materials but, sad to say, may sometimes be cannibalistic. They are

Black field crickets (*Gryllus*), male at left and female at right, are common almost everywhere. Only the males sing. They usually live on the ground in vegetation. Sometimes they are sold for fish bait.

easily reared in captivity, feeding upon a wide variety of foods, including ordinary dog food. As a result, many "cricket farms" are in operation, supplying live crickets to fishermen. In many instances these farms are large operations, producing millions of crickets each summer. These farm-reared crickets require from four to six weeks to reach bait size.

Unfortunately, black crickets often enter homes where they feed upon and destroy woolen goods, carpets, or clothing hanging in closets. I once witnessed a strange invasion of these insects into a southern town where they had congregated along the streets of the downtown area in large numbers. Some of them had entered clothing stores and damaged clothing, especially garments made of nylon.

In some parts of the Southeast there occurs a black cricket known as the short-tailed cricket *(Anurogryllus muticus)*. This insect ranges widely, being found as far south as Argentina. It is a serious pest in forests, where it destroys pine seedlings by

75

feeding upon the young needles. These crickets are the only ones that build multichambered burrows in the soil, never venturing above ground during the daylight hours. They live in their burrows, using some of the chambers for discarded food materials. Eggs are laid in the burrows and, after hatching, the young remain in the burrows for about a month, being fed and cared for by the females. Later, the young forage for food in the surrounding area. In Louisiana it was found that a number of spiders and mites live as guests, or *inquilines,* in the burrows along with the crickets.

For centuries, in Oriental lands, crickets have been kept in cages for their songs. The insects are carefully fed and the cages in which they are kept are often very attractive and elaborate. In some instances these cages are fashioned out of gourds grown especially for the purpose. While the gourds are small, they are inserted into bottles of various shapes. As the gourds grow, they gradually fill the bottles, assuming the shapes of the containers that enclose them. The bottles, of course, must be broken and the gourds removed and hollowed out. In some cases cricket cages are made of porcelain or ivory, fitted with lids of carved jade. The songs of the crickets were once so esteemed that cages of them were almost always kept in the royal palaces of the ancient Chinese empire.

Several different species of crickets have been caged in China for their songs. One of these is the besprinkled cricket *(Gryllus conspersus)*, another is the mitered cricket *(G. mitratus)*. The latter species has a call resembling the click of a weaver's shuttle and its Chinese name is *tsu-chi,* meaning "one who stimulates spinning." Another species is the broad-faced cricket *(Loxoblemmus tiacoun)*, known as the watchman's rattle, because of the sound of its call.

Since about 960 A.D., crickets have been kept and trained in

Le Quang Long

In Asiatic countries crickets have been reared and sold for thousands of years for their fighting abilities. Large sums are often bet on the contestants. This photograph shows cricket vendors on a street in Saigon.

Fighting crickets. Before a bout fighting crickets are twirled by their antennae to make them angry. One of the contestants is always killed. Le Quang Long

several Oriental countries for their fighting ability. This pastime is similar, in a way, to the fighting of game cocks in America. Many of our men in Viet Nam have seen these little insect gladiators battling with each other, the bouts sometimes taking place on street corners. In China this was formerly a national form of entertainment, and pedigrees were kept of crickets that showed outstanding fighting traits. These fighting crickets were fed special foods consisting of rice and boiled chestnuts as well as mosquitoes that had been allowed to gorge themselves with blood from their trainers' arms. All these foods, it was believed, helped to increase the crickets' fighting abilities. In addition, these fighting crickets' training included baths in concoctions of aromatic herbs and exercises consisting of being bounced up and down while tied to twigs.

Previous to entering the ring, the combatants were angered by being tickled with rat or hare whiskers set in bone or ivory handles. The fights usually ended in the death of the loser. Just as in American prize fights, the crickets were weighed-in on sensitive scales before each bout and each one fought in its own weight class designed as heavyweight, middleweight, and light-weight.

Closely related to the black crickets but unlike them in general appearance are the delicate tree crickets (Oecanthus). The technical name means "I dwell in flowers." These crickets are pale-green or whitish and are thus frequently known as snowy tree crickets. As their name indicates, they live in trees or shrubs and the females insert their eggs in bark or in the twigs of trees. When abundant this egg-laying may injure the trees. These are among the best of all insect musicians, the males tuning up at evening, or sometimes, on cloudy days.

In China and Japan, tree crickets of various kinds are especially esteemed as songsters. For example, the black tree cricket

78

(*Homoegryllus japonicus*) is known in China as the *kim chung*, meaning "golden bell," because its song resembles the tinkling sound of tiny bells. These crickets are unusual in that caged males will not sing unless females are caged with them.

THE CAVE CRICKETS AND CAMEL CRICKETS— FAMILY STENOPELMATIDAE

These peculiar insects are crickets of medium or large size. Their bodies are humpbacked and robust, and they are usually wingless. In color they are brownish or gray and have very long antennae. Sometimes these antennae are four or five times the length of the insects' bodies. Unusual is the fact that most of them are at least partly carnivorous, that is, their food is largely of animal origin. Very few kinds makes sounds.

The habits of the insects belonging to this family vary greatly and some are most uncommon. Among these are the cave crickets that spend their entire lives in the total darkness of deep caves. These crickets have unusually long antennae, no doubt a great advantage as sensory organs in their dark habitats. The hind legs of these crickets are very long, enabling them to hop for considerable distances. I have seen them deep in caves in Tennessee where they had no doubt lived for thousands of generations without seeing the light of day. These were the common cave crickets (*Hadenoecus subterraneus*). Their body color is yellowish-brown and their eyes are black. S. H. Scudder, in 1861, wrote of these strange crickets he had observed in Mammoth Cave, Kentucky. He says, "They were found throughout the cave to the remotest parts (seven miles or thereabouts), though not near the entrance . . . they were usually jumping about with the greatest alacrity upon the walls . . . they would leap away from approaching footsteps, but stop at a cessation of the noise, turning about and swaying their long antennae in a most ludicrous manner . . . The least noise would increase their tremulousness while they were unconcerned at distant motions unaccompanied by sound . . . neither did the light of the lamp appear to disturb them . . . Their eyes were perfectly formed and they could apparently see with ease, for they jump away from the slowly approaching hand."

My own limited experience with these remarkable crickets was similar to that of Mr. Scudder. It was, I found, almost impossible to collect perfect museum specimens because of their fragile structure.

Life in the utter darkness of subterranean caves has brought about several special adaptations in these insects. Their long antennae are, of course, a sensory asset. In order for the males and females to recognize each other the males have evolved scent glands on their abdomens. Certainly these cave crickets must depend upon senses other than sight to locate other members and to find food or avoid enemies such as bats.

So far I have been unable to discover what these crickets, living deep in caves, feed upon. Vernon Bailey, the naturalist, states that they are evidently scavengers. When he set traps for cave rats the crickets were a nuisance, since they not only fed upon the baits but nibbled at the trapped rats. Ultimately all food in deep caves comes from the outside, since green plants cannot grow there. However, rats and mice come and go, as do bats. Insects living deep in caves must feed upon each other or upon the waste material from animals that frequently leave the cave in search of outside food.

Surface streams, in many cases, disappear underground and flow through caves. In these streams dwell blind crayfish of pale coloration, as well as cave fish and salamanders. There are also blind beetles. The ones I saw in some Tennessee caves were

80

Cave crickets (*Ceuthophilus*) are wingless but have unusually long antennae and powerful hind, jumping legs. (Life size: 1 1/2 inches)

cream-colored and belonged to the family Carabidae. They were identified as *Anophthalmus*.

In addition to the cave cricket discussed above, there are several other cave-inhabiting species. One of these is the cave camel-cricket *(Ceuthophilus stygius)* which probably lives no deeper in caves than about half a mile. Often these crickets congregate in little groups on the walls, their heads all pointing inward as if the insects were holding a conference. Probably these crickets are blind, although eyes are present. They pay no attention to a lighted candle but are sensitive to heat or touch. When disturbed they may leap as far as six feet. Close relatives of this cave cricket have been found living in the underground burrows of gopher turtles in Florida. These unusual turtles burrow in sandy soil, emerging to feed upon surrounding vegetation. Their burrows are often fifteen to twenty feet long and may be located as deep as two or three feet below the surface of the ground.

The distribution of cave crickets and other cave-inhabiting insects is interesting, since they cannot exist for long in the outside world because they have become so completely adapted to cave life. In general there is no way for them to go from one cave to another unless the caves are connected. Thus cave insects are often confined to one cave or to neighboring caves. In the case of some insects, each cave has its own species of insect. The common cave cricket is found only in Mammoth Cave and in caves nearby. The cave camel-cricket is common in Indiana caves but is rare in Mammoth Cave. Cave crickets of other species are found only in Carlsbad Caverns, New Mexico.

There are a number of other, related, crickets found in America but they are all similar in habits and appearance to the cave crickets. They are humpbacked and are called camel crickets. Usually these insects are found in dark, damp places such as

82

Cave crickets often congregate on the walls of caves in large numbers. They are related to camel crickets.

basements, old wells, or under logs. In the Great Smoky Mountains I frequently found them under big stones. Sometimes they congregate in large numbers.

In Australia and New Zealand there are some unusual cave crickets of large size. The most common one in New Zealand is the cave weta *(Pachyrhamma acanthocera)* which has a total length, including the antennae, of nearly fourteen inches. It can jump for six feet. Another, the Australian king cricket *(Anostostoma australasiae)*, has extremely large jaws and its body measures about three inches in length.

In western United States there occur some peculiar members of this family known as Jerusalem or sand crickets *(Stenopelmatus)*. These insects are usually found under stones or in similar situations. They have large heads and apparently feed upon both plant and animal materials. There are several kinds.

New Zealand has a number of unusual insects. One of these is the strange tree weta *(Paragryllacris)*. These wingless crickets are about two inches long and the male has very large, powerful jaws with which it may bite severely. When angered, a tree weta waves its antennae about and raises its barbed hind legs over its head in a threatening maner. As these barbed legs are moved forward they are rubbed along the rough sides of the body making a sound like a match being struck. In bush areas where these insects are abundant the sound may often be heard at night as the wetas search for food.

THE MOLE CRICKETS—FAMILY GRYLLOTALPIDAE

The family name for these insects comes from two Latin words meaning "cricket mole," which is a very apt description of their habits and appearance. They live in the ground, often burrowing along just beneath the surface. These subsurface burrows may be seen from above, since they appear as meandering breaks on the surface of the ground. They actually are miniatures of mole tunnels and are made in the same way.

A mole cricket is about an inch and a half long and most unusual looking. Its front legs are stout and shovel-like, well fitted for tunneling through the ground. Anyone who looks at a mole cricket cannot help but be impressed by its resemblance to a mole. Here is a case where life in a similar habitat has resulted in similar form. The front digging legs of both cricket and mole are remarkably alike, and they both burrow through the soil, using their spadelike front legs to push aside the earth.

The front feet and legs of mole crickets resemble four-pronged spading forks and also function like shears for cutting

84

Mole crickets burrow in the ground, often just below the surface, using their spadelike front feet. They feed upon plant roots. (Life size: 1 1/2 inches)

A mole cricket's front legs are modified in a remarkable way to enable it to tunnel through the ground. One portion of the foot moves across the bladelike teeth after the fashion of a hedge clipper. In this way it cuts small roots.

A mole cricket burrow in sand in the Everglades. The insect has tunneled along just below the surface.

small roots. When in water, these flattened legs serve as oars to propel the insect. The Cherokee Indians were evidently close observers; they noticed that the insect had seven finger-like projections on each front leg. As a result, it was called *gul kwagi*, meaning "seven." They also believed that if the tongue of a slow-learning child was scratched with the claw of a living mole cricket its intelligence would be improved.

Sometimes these crickets leave their burrows and fly. The males have well-developed sound-making organs with which they make gruff chirps that are probably used as recognition sounds in their underground burrows.

I have often seen mole cricket burrows in the damp earth or sand along streams. Deep in the Everglades of Florida I studied their habits, sometimes watching them at night with a flashlight. It was an eerie setting in an area where bears were common and where the bellows of bull alligators echoed from the nearby marshes. Upon the ground in the rays of my flashlight I watched as the crickets tunneled along, pushing up little windrows in the sandy soil. Sometimes a cricket would push its head up above the surface, perhaps to observe the surroundings; then it would retreat into its tunnel and burrow along again. When I visited the area the next morning I noticed that birds had been busy probing along the crickets' tunnels in search of them. The birds, probably some kind of shore birds, had left their telltale tracks in the soft sand.

The tunnels made by mole crickets are permanent runways used for considerable periods, and may extend for several inches below the surface. It is in these deeper burrows that the eggs are laid, usually a total of about thirty-five, placed in several separate chambers. They are laid in spring and require more than a month to hatch. There is but one generation a year.

Since a mole cricket may cover several square yards of soil surface in a single night, making its typical raised ridges, it may often injure many young plants, especially if its activity is located in seed beds or gardens. For this reason they are considered to be pests in some localities. In any case, they are unusual and interesting insects and there are four kinds found in the United States. Most abundant is the common mole cricket (*Gryllotalpa gryllotalpa*). Mole crickets of other kinds occur in several other parts of the world. In Australia and Patagonia are found some small, wingless relatives of these insects that burrow into the stems of plants.

THE ANT-LOVING CRICKETS—FAMILY MYRMECOPHILIDAE

Among the world's most unusual crickets are those that live with ants, sharing their living quarters and their food. In many cases they are treated almost like pets by the ants. These crickets are very small, wingless, and without hearing or sound-making organs. Their hind legs, however, are large and powerful, ena-

Tiny crickets of several kinds have taken up life with ants. They are tolerated by the ants and, seemingly, treated almost like pets. This one (right) lived with black carpenter ants.

bling them to jump away from the jaws of their hosts.

Insects living with ants are called *myrmecophiles,* meaning "ant-lovers." However, this name does not describe their true relationship to the ants. Some of the insects that live with ants are really parasites, feeding upon the ants' young. In any case, they are "star-boarders," sponging on the ants' hospitality. Some kinds secrete substances much desired by the ants and the relationship may almost be compared to drug addiction. In addition to crickets, there are ant-loving beetles, bugs, and other small insects.

Ant-loving crickets are of several kinds. I have found them associated with the large, black carpenter ants *(Camponotus)* that live in rotten wood. I also found them in the underground nests of fire ants *(Solenopsis)* and harvester ants *(Pogomomyrmex).* The interesting thing is that the size of these little crickets seems to be related to the size of the ants they are associated with; the larger the ants, the larger the crickets that live with them.

When an ant nest is broken into, these crickets, never very abundant, may be seen hopping about in a very agile manner. Thus, they are difficult to capture.

These crickets seem to live safely with the ants, often nibbling oily secretions from their bodies. In cages I have watched the ants being "groomed" by their guest crickets. Often the ants became irritated by the crickets and would snap at them with their jaws. However, the crickets always seemed able to jump away from harm and save themselves.

Ant-loving crickets have been living with ants for so long that they are unable to live anywhere else. There are a number of kinds; some live with ants of several species, others are associated with only one kind of ant.

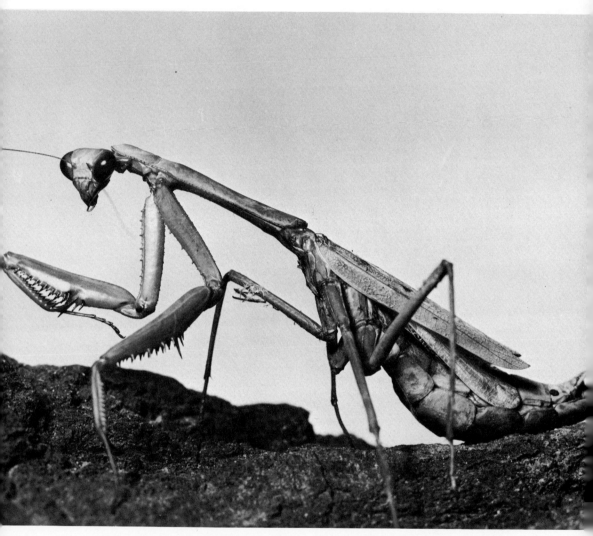

The praying mantis is one of nature's most voracious beasts. With its spiny front legs it can capture and devour almost any insect smaller than itself. This is the Carolina mantis (*Stagmomantis carolina*). (Life size: 3 inches)

CHAPTER **6**

THE MANTIS,
INSECT TIGER

The mantid (or mantis)—family Mantidae—lives by capturing and devouring other insects. It is, in truth, the most voracious predator of the entire insect world, a world where the usual rule is "eat or be eaten." No beast of the jungle has an appetite exceeding that of a mantis; any insect—or other small animal—so unfortunate as to stray too near to one of these creatures will almost certainly be killed and devoured. And the strange thing is that the mantis need not be really hungry at the time. We cannot say that a mantis kills for the pure joy of killing because, unlike humans, insects do not register joy or anger as we know these emotions. It is, in a way, a mechanical monster whose predatory reactions are stimulated by the mere presence of prey. I once fed several small grasshoppers to a mantis, a full meal, considering the insect's size. Yet, when I held an additional grasshopper in range of its raptorial front legs, it at once seized the still-living grasshopper and began feeding upon it. The nearest part of the grasshopper to the mantid's jaws was a leg, which the little monster nonchalantly began eating. When the leg was consumed, the rest of the hopper was slowly eaten until only the wings remained.

The above episode is recounted in detail to portray the mantis as it really is, a creature whose feeding reactions are triggered by the mere presence of food, not by actual hunger.

The insects belonging to this family are elongate in form, usually winged, whose front legs are modified into efficient organs for grasping and holding prey. When at rest these legs are held in front of the insect's body, making it appear as if it were in an attitude of prayer. In truth, the name mantis is derived from two Greek words meaning "prophet-like." Sometimes these insects are also known as soothsayers or praying mantids, both names referring to their supposed attitude of prayer. Many other names have been given them, including "rear-horses" and "devil-horses." The Arabs thought that they always prayed with their faces turned toward Mecca, and, in some lands, they are called "nuns," "mendicants," or "preachers." In Germany they are known as *Fangheuschrecken* (praying crickets) or *Gottesanbeterinnen* (worshipers of God). In Australia they are known as "forest ladies." The truth, of course, is that none of these names indicates the true nature of the mantis; to my mind, some other name, perhaps "devil insect," would be far more fitting.

Everything about a mantis is concerned with its habit of capturing and eating prey. Its eyes are large and its vision excellent. A captive specimen seems acutely aware of what is going on around it; it can move its head in all directions, watching any nearby movement. They make excellent photographic subjects, remaining quietly posed on a leaf or twig, and moving their heads about, watching the activities of the photographer. When alarmed, which is not often, they may walk away or take flight. They have no ears and no sound-making organs.

A praying mantis can take a lot of punishment and still live.

92

When hunting, a mantis approaches its prey very slowly. When within striking distance the forelegs snap out and grasp it.

I once had a specimen in captivity whose head had been accidentally severed. The strange thing was that it lived for several days in my laboratory, walking about in a very normal fashion. Edwin Way Teale, the nature writer, recounts a similar experience.

In its native habitat a mantis will devour, or attempt to do so, almost any creature it can grasp in its formidable front legs. Studies have been made of these remarkable grasping legs and the results analyzed by electronic computers. In these tests it was found that the mantids were most apt to respond by striking at prey of medium size; that is, prey measuring about one-fourth inch in diameter and seven-eighths inch in length, the size of

93

prey a mantis is most apt to encounter. They responded least to very small or very large prey. These tests also revealed that a mantid's grasping legs were so designed, or adapted, as to afford maximum grasping ability when prey of the above size is captured.

If you are interested in specific details, the two grasping joints of the leg (femur and tibia) are hinged, allowing them to be folded together in a manner similar to the way the human thumb and forefinger oppose each other when a ball is grasped in the hand. The forces generated as the fingers are brought together operate at right angles to tangents of the ball's circular surface. This generates a frictional force illustrated by a line drawn from the bases of the fingers and passing through the center of the ball. The ball will be held between thumb and forefinger just so long as the frictional force is greater than the force causing the ball to slip from between the fingers. Thus, a golf ball may be held tightly, while a baseball tends to slip from between the fingers. The same thing occurs when a mantis captures an insect; if it is a large insect it will tend to slip out of the grasping leg and escape. The efficiency of the mantid's grasping mechanism is, of course, increased by the presence of teeth located along the inner surfaces of the two segments of the leg. When prey is captured the curving hook at the outer end of the tibia helps to prevent it from slipping or rolling outward and escaping. Thus, the leg of the mantis is especially adapted to the capture of prey of a certain, average, size. All this may sound quite technical but it does demonstrate how well these insects have become adapted to the capture of their normal prey—flies, small grasshoppers, and other medium-sized insects.

While the above research shows how nicely these remarkable insects are fitted to the capture of prey, they will often capture, or attempt to capture, much smaller or much larger animals.

94

Once prey, such as this luckless katydid, is captured, it is slowly eaten. Only the wings remain undevoured.

They have been known to prey upon small frogs, lizards, butterflies, spiders, and bumblebees. In one case a small turtle was attacked. In another instance, a mantis was discovered clutching a short-tailed shrew which it had presumably captured. In short, a mantis will attempt to capture and eat any creature that does not capture it first. There is one strange thing, however, that I must mention; mantids seems to be afraid of ants! Why, I do not know.

It is always fascinating to watch a mantid capture its prey. I have done so many times and have always marveled at its technique. It is a technique that I have successfully copied in capturing such alert insects as robber flies. If a robber fly is found perched on a plant and the fingers move very slowly toward it, the fly may be picked up by closing the fingers quickly when they are almost upon the fly. This is possible because the insect's eyes are especially adapted to perceiving motion; slowly moving

95

objects do not appear to alarm it. When a mantid sees a fly or other likely prey it moves slowly toward it, sometimes swaying its body from side to side. Its actions remind one of the way in which a cat stalks a mouse. When within striking distance, the mantid's two front legs flash out and the luckless insect is captured and the mantis at once begins feeding upon it. The mantis is probably the only insect whose head may be moved freely in order to see in all directions. When perched on a twig, one of these insects will move its head about, apparently observing everything that goes on in its vicinity. As in most insects, mantids have compound eyes, that is, eyes made up of many small, separate eyes, each with a separate lens. In some insects, such as bees, only light from a source directly in front of each separate eye can enter and be registered in the insect's brain. In the case of the mantis and a few other insects, light entering the individual lenses may cross to adjacent light-sensitive nerve endings, enabling them to see in dim light.

Like the majority of insects, a mantid is capable of very rapid motion, especially when striking at prey with its front legs. As in many insects, including flies, the mantid has a few "giant fibers" running the entire length of its nervous system. These fibers are capable of carrying impulses very rapidly in order to bring about quick action. Thus, a fly may respond to an alarm in about a twentieth of a second, the same time required for a mantis to complete the act of striking at it. However, in spite of the fact that both insects respond at approximately the same rate, the mantis can usually capture a fly.

So far we have omitted mentioning the most gruesome of all mantid habits. Mating occurs in late summer or autumn when they are full grown. The male is, seemingly, very foolish or, perhaps, stupid to approach the female of his choice. She is larger than he is and more powerful. However, driven by the

So voracious are mantids that it is not unusual for the female to devour the male after mating with him.

mating urge, the male mantid approaches the female and mating occurs. For the male this is often fatal since the lady usually devours him when it is over. So bloodthirsty is she that, in many cases, she commences her cannibal feast during the mating act. However, we must remember that in Nature's economy the male is thus serving an additional useful purpose; his body is furnishing nourishment for the eggs developing within the female's body. Winter is not far away and he will shortly die anyway or be captured by some bird.

Soon after mating the female locates a suitable twig. It is not known how she determines its suitability, but she rests quietly upon the twig, head downwards. Soon a frothy material begins issuing from the tip of her abdomen as she moves it slowly about. At the same time eggs pour out of her oviducts and into the mass of froth which begins to harden. When the froth has become firm, it forms a protective covering for the eggs, making them safe from birds and most other enemies during the winter months.

With the arrival of springs the eggs begin hatching and the tiny mantids come out of their protective case. Even at this young and tender age they exhibit the same voracious character-istics as their elders. They feed upon tiny insects such as aphids and begin growing. If these mantid egg-masses are collected in winter and brought indoors they may hatch before spring, mak-ing the feedings of the young quite difficult in the absence of aphids. Thus, it is best to keep collected mantid egg-masses in a refrigerator until the weather turns warm. As in the case of other insects, mantids grow by shedding their skins several times dur-ing development.

In the world there are more than 1,500 species of mantids,

Mantids deposit their masses of eggs on twigs where they remain until spring be-fore hatching.

When alarmed, a mantis may spread its wings and fly. A moment after this picture was taken this Carolina mantis flew away.

most of which are found in tropical lands. They are especially abundant in Africa. Only fifteen kinds are found in the United States. Mantids of most kinds live in trees but a few are ground-dwelling. The most common and best known North American mantid is the Carolina mantid *(Stagmomantis carolina)* which ranges from the Gulf states north to New York and westward to Arizona. The female is greenish-yellow, with a dark spot on each front wing. She measures about two and one-fourth inches in length. The male is smaller, measuring only about two inches and is grayish in color. The egg-masses of this mantid are about an inch long with the eggs arranged in parallel rows set at an inclined angle. The young usually emerge in May.

Common also in many places is the European mantis *(Mantis religiosa)*, a species that was accidentally introduced into this country about 1899 near Rochester, New York. Apparently it entered the country in egg-masses attached to nursery stock.

It is pale green and about two inches in length. Another mantid of foreign origin is the Chinese mantid *(Paratenodera sinensis)*, native to China and Japan. This one is very long and slender, and green in color. It measures about four inches long. It was first discovered in the United States near Philadelphia about 1896 and has since spread to most of the eastern states. It is especially abundant in the South, and is also found in Hawaii. Most of the other mantids in the United States are smaller than those mentioned above.

In tropical areas there are some mantids of colorful and remarkable form. Among these are the bark mantids of Australia that mimic the color of bark upon which they usually live. Some kinds resemble ants.

The Oriental region seems to possess some of the world's most remarkable species, many of which are masters of camouflage and illusion. One of these is the rose-leaf mantis of India that has been known and marveled at by entomologists for several hundred years. These insects have leaflike expansions on the prothorax (the body segment just back of the head) and other, similar, expansions on their legs. When viewed from above these expansions are green but, from below, are lavender-violet with a pinkish bloom along the edges. This form and coloration makes the mantid resemble a flower. The illusion is completed by a dark blotch that simulates the opening of the corolla tube of a flower. These amazing insects remain motionless among the foliage, now and then swaying their bodies as if moved by a breeze. Insects tricked by the flower-like appearance of the mantid are lured to it, seeking nectar. This, of course, is a fatal error, since they are almost certain to be captured and devoured by the "flower."

In Malaysia there dwells another remarkable mantid *(Hymenopus coronatus)*, known to the natives as the *kanchong*,

100

The slender Asiatic mantis, left, (*Paratenodera sinensis*) devours a long-horned grasshopper while its American cousin, the Carolina mantis, looks on. (Life size of Asiatic mantis: 4 inches)

which mimics a pink orchid. When insects such as butterflies are attracted to this "wolf in flower's clothing" they are captured and eaten. The entire insect is colored and shaped to resemble the orchids among which it hides. To its legs are attached pink, petal-like expansions, completing the illusion that it is a bloom. The coloration and texture of this mantid resemble a blossom so closely that it is difficult to tell where "mantis leaves off and flower begins."

Africa, also, has a number of flower-mimicking mantids. One of these is the devil-flower mantid (*Idolum diabolicum*). Like some of its Oriental relatives, this mantid has leaflike body and leg-expansions, making it difficult to see when resting among flowers.

Along the Pilcomayo River in South America there occur some strange mantids almost perfectly camouflaged to resemble

101

lichen-covered bark. Unless they move, these insects are quite difficult to spot. In this same region are found some small mantids that mimic bird droppings. Along the great Amazon River live some mantids having less than ethical habits. These are, in truth, "wolves in sheep's clothing." They resemble walking-stick insects so closely that only an expert can tell the difference. These sticklike mantids associate themselves with groups of walking-stick insects and capture them at their leisure, the rest of the walking-sticks being none the wiser when one of their number is devoured.

While mantids are among Nature's most voracious creatures, it is perhaps fitting that they should also have a number of insect enemies. Mantid egg-masses, even though well protected by their gluelike coating, are often fed upon by ants of several kinds. Ants also capture young mantids just out of the eggs. In addition, a number of tiny wasps live as parasites within the eggs. One kind of parasitic wasp *(Rielia manticida)* uses an interesting trick to locate a mantid's egg-mass. This little wasp, which is only about a tenth of an inch long, finds a female mantid and lights upon it, usually at the base of its wings where it cannot be reached by the mantid's grasping legs or jaws. Here the wasp gnaws off her own wings, no longer having need of them, and settles down to wait. When the mantid, at last, lays her mass of eggs the wasp crawls upon it and deposits her own eggs in those of the mantis. The mantid thus preyed upon is the common European species *(Mantis religiosa)*.

Yet another insect with the nerve to prey upon the mantis is a hunting wasp, a wasp similar to those that capture flies, grasshoppers, and other defenseless insects. Why a wasp would elect to prey upon the terrible mantis is an interesting question. As John Crompton so aptly says, "It is as if a man with rabbits and game in abundance all around sought, when he went out to get something to eat, only grizzly bears."

This young mantis poses on a pencil. Even at this age it is a voracious hunter of small insects.

This wasp *(Tachytes)* is hardly half an inch long, yet she specializes in mantids. She locates a mantis and hovers about it, darting at it now and then. In time the mantis tires or, perhaps, becomes careless. In any case, the wasp eventually darts down and grasps the mantid's necklike prothorax with her legs. Then, with lightening-like speed, she plunges her sting into the body of the mantis, which at once becomes unconscious. The wasp's next act is that of dragging the body of the mantis into her burrow where it will serve as food for her young. The moral here, perhaps, is that no matter how well an insect is adapted to the defense and the capture of prey, some other insect is apt to find a means of preying upon it.

So there you have the story of the mantid clan, the most ravenous and gluttonous of all insects and endowed with a bag full of tricks for enticing other small creatures within range of their grasping legs and jaws. When watching one of these little monsters in the act of capturing an insect I have often wondered what it would be like to encounter, in some forest, a mantis-like beast the size of a tiger. How glad I am that there exist no such nightmare creatures, even in the most remote and unknown reaches of the Amazonian jungle.

103

This giant walking-stick (*Megaphasma*) is the largest insect found in the United States. It occurs in the East. (Life size: 6 inches)

CHAPTER 7

THE WALKING-STICKS

These strange insects, in the prosaic language of entomologists, are described as "nonsaltatorial (nonjumping) Orthoptera." This, of course, is true as far as it goes, but tells little about these peculiar grasshopper relatives that are classified in the family Phasmatidae. The name is of Greek origin meaning "a ghost" or "specter."

The most obvious characteristic of a walking-stick insect is its resemblance to a twig or a stick. When resting or quietly feeding among foliage they are very difficult to see, so closely do they mimic a twig. This mimicry is so complete that even the joints and thorns of the twigs are reproduced on the insect's body and limbs. Several kinds are probably quite common yet are seen only by accident, due probably to their form and lethargic habits. They are, to our forests, what tree sloths are to the jungles of Central and South America, defenseless creatures that survive by remaining quietly in trees, feeding upon the foliage.

Walking-sticks are remarkable for their resemblance to twigs; their bodies are elongate, very slender, and their eyes are small.

105

Walking-sticks mimic twigs, making them difficult to see. They live among tree leaves upon which they feed. This one has lost one front leg (Life size: 5 inches)

Keen vision is unnecessary to creatures that lead sedentary lives and have little or no means of defending themselves. If a walking-stick happens to be spotted by a bird or other enemy it cannot move swiftly enough to escape. Often a walking-stick will feign death or "play possum." This is one of their peculiar habits. They belong to the clan of the hunted, rather than the hunters.

I am always impressed by creatures that live by hunting; they are agile and alert, and have keen vision. I recall a time when

106

I watched a falcon perched on its nest high up on the face of a cliff of the Rockies. Through a powerful telescope I could see its piercing eyes surveying the river and the valley stretching away below, eyes that calmly watched swallows circling in the sky above and a marmot sunning itself upon a boulder far down the mountainside. I was certain, too, that even at that great distance, the falcon noted with interest the domestic hens in the barnyard of the ranch along the river. Like the mantis, the falcon is a hunter and its acute vision enables it to spot its prey. What a contrast there is between the hunters and the hunted, between the tiger and the cow, between the mantis and the walking-stick. Mantis and walking-stick are both orthopterans, yet one lives by the hunt, the other is a slow-moving eater of leaves.

I suspect that walking-sticks are much more common, especially in eastern forests, than is usually supposed. Some are known to become so abundant as to cause severe damage to trees by their feeding. Due to their concealing form and sluggish actions, people seldom see them.

One kind of walking-stick is our largest native insect. This is the giant walking-stick (*Megaphasma dentricus*). The generic name *Megaphasma*, means "a large apparition or ghost," and the name is quite appropriate. One of these creatures measures about six inches long and its body resembles a small branch with twigs (its legs) sprouting out of it. When resting and feeding among leaves it moves very little, and then only from one leaf to another with slow, deliberate motions. It usually lives and feeds in oak forests but, in Texas, was found to be common on wild grape vines.

Like most walking-sticks, this giant drops its eggs to the ground, where they rest among fallen leaves until the next spring or, perhaps, the second spring before hatching. These eggs are about one-eighth inch in length and, under a hand lens, look

107

like tiny hand grenades. The eggs of other walking-sticks resemble seeds; as a matter of fact, the eggs of some kinds are almost indistinguishable from the seeds of the plants or trees upon which they live.

Probably the most widespread of all walking-sticks is the common walking-stick (*Diapheromera femorata*) that sometimes reaches a length of more than three inches in the case of the female. Generally speaking, female walking-sticks are considerably larger than the males. The common walking-stick usually feeds upon the leaves of oak or wild cherry. It has the habit of stretching its body along a twig, making it very difficult to spot. In eastern North America it ranges all the way from southern Canada to New Mexico.

Rather common in some localities are the striped walking-stick (*Anisomorpha buprestoides*) and the lesser striped walking-stick (*A. ferruginea*). The larger species is found in Florida and

Left: The eggs of the giant walking-stick resemble tiny hand grenades. They are dropped to the ground where they remain until the following spring before hatching. (Life size: 1/8 inch) Right: Eggs of the *Anisomorpha* walking-stick. Their coloration and form make them difficult to see on the ground among dead leaves. (Life size: 1/8 inch)

Here a giant walking-stick feeds upon a leaf. So effective is their camouflage that they are rarely seen.

other southeastern states, while the lesser species ranges over most of the eastern half of the United States. These are robust, heavy-bodied insects that have the habit of squirting an acid, milklike fluid from their bodies when picked up. This is doubtless used as a defense against enemies such as birds or, perhaps, other insects. It is because of this secretion that these walking-sticks are sometimes called "musk-mares."

While striped walking-sticks usually live in the foliage of trees and bushes, I have often found them clinging to the bark or trunks. They are especially active at night. The female of the larger striped walking-stick is about two and one-half inches

109

The female of this walking-stick (*Anisomorpha*) is much larger than the male. Her body is swollen with eggs. This pair was photographed in the mating act. (Life size, female: 2 inches)

long, while the female of the lesser species is somewhat smaller. The males of both species are much smaller, usually only about half the size of the females. In the strange case of a European walking-stick, the females reproduce without mating, that is, young are produced by *parthenogenesis*. Males occur, but are rare and are apparently not capable of mating.

While all of the walking-sticks found on the mainland of the United States are wingless, there is a winged form, known as Mayer's walking-stick *(Aplopus mayeri)* that has been collected on several of the Florida keys. It is a tropical species, probably also inhabiting the West Indies. Its wings are too small for flight.

All of the walking-sticks found in the United States are of

110

This green walking-stick insect from the Philippine Islands has wings that resemble leaves. On its legs are green, leaf-like expansions. (Life size: 3 inches)

sticklike form, but in many tropical lands, there are several that have leaflike leg and body expansions that make them resemble leaves. Some of these remind one of certain leaflike mantids. They are green in color and mimic leaves, even to the presence of veins. They occur in Polynesia, Africa, and Oriental areas where their native names may be translated as "walking leaves" or "leaf insects." In Australia, walking-sticks are often so abundant as to damage eucalyptus forests. It is said that their eggs, falling upon the dry leaves beneath the trees, sound like rain. Some tropical kinds are colored and mottled to resemble spiny twigs, mosses, and lichens. Some of these tropical walking-sticks are more than a foot in length.

Cockroaches were among the first insects to fly. They have changed but little down the eons.

CHAPTER **8**

COCKROACHES,
THE ANCIENT INSECTS

Once upon a time, as the storybooks say, much of the world had a warm, tropical climate and was clothed with luxuriant vegetation consisting of treelike ferns, giant horsetails, and other plants not found in the modern world. Just as today, there were lakes and streams, but over them darted great dragonflies nearly a yard across. In the forests dwelled strange beasts. All this, of course, was far in the distant past, about 300 million years ago. Known to scientists as the Carboniferous Period, is was the time when the coal beds were being formed by the slow accumulation of half-decayed vegetation. This plant debris would eventually be covered by sediments and gradually compressed and changed chemically, resulting in the coal beds we know today. This period of earth history was also the heyday of the cockroach clan.

We may not appreciate the lowly cockroaches, usually regarding them as disgusting insects with filthy habits. However, the truth is that they have an ancient lineage extending far back

113

This giant cockroach is common in the jungles of Panama. Its ancestors lived in Carboniferous forests, millions of years ago. (Life size: 3 inches)

down the halls of time. They come from an "old family." Their ancestors were probably the first of all creatures to possess wings. Thus, their ability to fly antedates by millions of years that of both birds and bats. Cockroaches probably reached their peak of abundance during the late Carboniferous. Based on the relative number of fossils found, it is believed that at that time they constituted more than 70 per cent of the insects that lived, as contrasted to only 3.4 per cent today. Some authorities do not agree; they maintain that the high percentage of cockroaches during the Carboniferous, as indicated by the numerous fossils, is misleading. It is their opinion that more cockroaches were fossilized at that time because these insects mostly lived in the moist, swampy areas and so more of them were apt to be pre-

114

served as fossils. In any case, we may rest assured that there were numerous cockroaches living then.

While cockroaches have gradually disappeared from the world scene, leaving but a fragment of their former numbers, they and their ancestors had an important place in insect evolution. They bequeathed to insects the heritage of wings, probably one of the most important events in their long, slow evolution.

Several million years passed and the Permian Period dawned. Climates were then dry, the seas were draining away from the continents, and the first coniferous trees appeared. The insect legions were on the rise; many new types came into being. Some of these ancient insects were much larger than those now living and many of them left their fossilized remains in many parts of the world. Some, including the cockroaches, became entrapped in the resin of trees. This resin slowly hardened into amber, preserving the trapped insects in remarkable detail. Some of them

When held in the hand with its wings spread, the Panama cockroach's size is evident.

Nymphal cockroaches are wingless. During later stages the wings appear, although some kinds remain wingless.

look as if they had been alive only yesterday rather than millions of years ago.

The oldest known insect fossil is that of a cockroach (*Paleoblatta douvillei*) that was found in sandstone in France, laid down during the Silurian Period nearly 400 million years ago. Since so many fossilized cockroaches have been found, we know more about their ancestry than about any other group of insects. The fact is, however, that in their long evolutionary history, roaches have changed very little, yet the study of them has aided in piecing together our knowledge of the evolution of all other insect groups.

Cockroaches belong to the insect family Blattidae, from the Latin *blatta*, an "insect that shuns the light." These insects are known in almost every land except those that are too cold for them to survive. They have many names, including croton bugs and water-bugs. In Germany they are called *Schaben*, in France

116

This is the same species of roach as in the last picture, the winged adult. (Life size: 1 1/2 inches)

les blattes, and, in Spanish lands, *cucarachas.* They were known to the American Indians, who have a number of superstitions regarding them. For example, it was believed that these insects were valuable in the cure of whooping cough. A cockroach was placed in a container and when it died the afflicted child was supposed to be cured.

A typical roach is flattened, has a tough, brownish body, and can run very rapidly. Many kinds have wings and often take to the air. However, there are numerous cockroaches that are completely wingless. In some cases the females have very short wings, while males have fully developed wings. While a typical roach is brownish or black, some tropical species are quite colorful, being brilliant green, yellow, red, or other gay colors. The basal segments of their legs are unusually large and almost completely cover the underside of the body. Some kinds have glands that secrete odorous substances.

Cockroach eggs are not laid individually as in the case of most other insects. Instead, the eggs are usually enclosed in a purselike case which is carried about for a time attached to the tip of the female's abdomen. This egg case is called an *oötheca* and is eventually dropped in some dark, or otherwise suitable, place where the eggs hatch. In some cases the eggs are retained within the female's body until they hatch. Thus, these young are born alive.

In feeding habits, cockroaches are usually omniverous, that is, they will eat almost anything. They are, in truth, scavengers. Those that live in human habitations are well adapted to invading kitchens and eluding housewives. Not only are they found in huts of natives in tropical lands but in kitchens of the finest homes. They find ships ideal as places to live and so have been carried to almost all parts of the globe. This was especially true in the days of sailing ships. Not often seen during the day, they come out of cracks and crevices at night and scurry about in search of food, their flattened bodies enabling them to find hiding places almost everywhere. Since they can run very rapidly they are usually able to escape capture.

In the world there are about 2,250 species, most of which live in the tropics. Many people seem to think that roaches live only in human habitations but the truth is that most kinds live in forests; only a few have found life with man to their liking. Some "wild" roaches have very unusual habits. In the East Indies is found a roach *(Rhicnoda natatrix)* that lives near water and often dives and hides in the bottoms of ponds and streams. Most remarkable of all roaches are those that have taken up life in the nests of ants, living there as if they were honored guests. One kind of these little "guest" roaches I had the pleasure of studying firsthand.

In southern Louisiana I was observing and photographing the

Cockroaches' eggs are enclosed in cases or oötheca which are carried about for a time. Eventually the egg case is dropped in a dark place.

This close-up of a cockroach egg case shows the details of its structure. It is brown in color. (Life size: 1/4 inch)

At least one kind of cockroach has taken up life with ants. The tiny cockroach (*Attaphila fungicola*) at left lives in the nests of tropical leaf-cutting ants (*Atta*). (Life size: 1/16 inch)

remarkable leaf-cutting ants *(Atta)* that cut sections out of leaves and carry them into large underground cavities where they serve as a compost upon which the ants grow a special fungus as food. I had dug downward through the sandy soil to a depth of nearly eight feet before locating one of the cavities where the ants had their fungus garden. The cavity was about the size and shape of a small watermelon and nearly filled with the grayish fungus. In the process of examining this fungus garden, I was pleased to find several of the tiny guest cockroaches *(Attaphila fungicola)*. They were very small, hardly one-eighth inch long, and wingless. These minute roaches apparently feed upon secretions from the ants' bodies, not upon the fungus grown by them. The strange thing is that every roach found in one of these ant nests has had its antennae cut off. Why this is, no one seems to know.

Least expected, perhaps, is the fact that cockroaches are among

120

the most "intelligent" of insects. It has been found that they have considerable learning ability. Normally, roaches always escape by darting into the safety of cracks or other dark places. In a famous experiment, carried out many years ago, roaches received a mild electrical shock each time they entered a dark box. This must have been very frustrating to the insects, but after repeating their attempts to enter the dark box several times they eventually learned to avoid the box. They would stop excitedly at the entrance and turn back into the light, not a roach's normal reaction at all. These roaches had learned that there was danger

Cockroaches have excellent eyesight even though they are active mostly at night: Some kinds fly toward bright lights.

Cockroaches of most kinds dwell in forests and jungles. They are especially abundant in the tropics. This woodland roach lived in the Great Smoky Mountains. (Life size: 1 inch)

in the dark rather than refuge. However, they had short memories; they "forgot" about the shocks after only one hour and again ran into the darkened box. In these tests it was discovered that the males learned a little more quickly than the females.

One of the ways in which biologists study insects' and other animals' learning abilities is by placing them in complicated mazes. These are passages having several blind endings and choice-points, and an animal's learning ability is gauged by the number of trials and the time required to learn its way through. In such experiments it was found that after only five or six runs through a maze most roaches reached the end with fewer errors and made better time than they had made in the first trial. However, there was a difference in learning abilities of various kinds of roaches. Oriental roaches (*Blatta orientalis*), for exam-

122

Cockroaches, like most insects, grow by shedding their outer skins several times. This roach was photographed in the act of shedding its skin. At first the roach is white. Later, it will turn dark brown.

ple, have short memories and had to be retrained each day. American roaches *(Periplaneta americana)* not only remembered from one day to the next but improved after several days. In similar tests another facet of cockroach psychology came to light. If two or three roaches were placed together in a maze they learned more slowly than if they had been alone. Seemingly, the presence of other roaches had a distracting influence on their ability to learn.

Cockroaches have been the subjects of numerous other experiments. For example, it has been found that if they are kept continuously in a dark room, they become active when night arrives outside. Thus, a roach need not see that darkness has come to go out on its nightly prowl. It was found that a hormone or chemical substance released in the head every twenty-four hours

123

"tells" the insect that the time has come to leave its hiding place and to go out in search of food.

While most cockroaches live in forests, where they hide under rotten logs, or under rocks, or in similar places, there are a few that have taken up residence in human habitations. The most common of these will be discussed below.

THE AMERICAN ROACH (PERIPLANETA AMERICANA)

This is the largest of our domestic pest roaches, measuring more than one and one-half inches in length. It is native to Mexico and Central America and is also common in the South. It has been accidentally carried by ships to almost all parts of the world. It has well-developed wings and often flies to lights.

THE BROWN ROACH (PERIPLANETA BRUNNEA)

These are large in size, usually about an inch in length. In color they range from dark brown to almost black. They are common in the South, where they live outside, sometimes entering homes.

THE ORIENTAL ROACH (BLATTA ORIENTALIS)

These are large, dark-colored cockroaches, about one inch in length. The males are winged but the females are wingless. They prefer damp basements or kitchens. It is believed by several authorities that this roach, along with the so-called American roach, came to America originally from Africa on slave ships. The Oriental roach is found in the wild state in Africa. It is found also in Europe where it is believed to have arrived in Phoenician ships in ancient times. Later it appeared in both North and South America.

124

THE GERMAN ROACH (BLATTELLA GERMANICUS)

These are probably the best known and most widespread of all pest roaches. This insect is probably a native of Europe but has followed man to all parts of the earth. Much smaller than the ones previously discussed, it measures only about one-half inch in length and is pale yellowish-brown in color. Both sexes are winged. Sometimes they are known as water-bugs or croton bugs.

THE BROWN-BANDED ROACH (SUPELLA SUPELLECTILIUM)

These are about the same size as the German roach, brown in color, but marked with two pale bands across the base of the wings and another band across the wings a third of the way back. Unlike most other domestic roaches, it prefers to live in shelves, closets, desks, and in starched curtains. Thus, it may be found in any part of the home.

THE DEATH'S-HEAD ROACH (BLABERUS CRANIFER)

This tropical species is the largest roach found in the United States. It measures nearly two and one-half inches in length and has markings on its prothorax resembling a skull. It occurs in Florida.

A katydid (*Microcentrum*) raises its front wings when singing. The wings are moved in and out very rapidly.

CHAPTER 9

THEIR SONGS

No sound is more characteristic of a summer evening in the country than the songs of insects. To give a feeling of night in the out-of-doors, television sound-effects engineers almost always dub in recordings of crickets or katydids.

Most insects are silent but many, including numerous orthopterans, have well-developed sound-making equipment. There are three chief ways that insects produce sound. One way is by expelling air forcibly from the spiracles or air vents along the sides of their bodies. This results in a hissing sound and is found in a few cockroaches and in the large lubber grasshoppers. Cockroaches of the genus *Gromphadorhina* found in Madagascar produce such hissing sounds and are so clearly heard that Europeans living there call them "blowers." These unusual roaches hiss for various reasons; males do so in defense of territories or when courting, females also hiss but usually in defense of young. The second method of sound production used by insects is that of snapping a membrane in and out by means of special muscles attached to its inner surface. In effect, this is similar to the way a drum emits sound except that, in the case of the drum, the membrane or "head" is caused to vibrate by being struck with a drumstick. Such drumming organs are found in cicadas. The third, and most common, sound-making technique is that of rubbing one part of the body against another part. This friction-type method of sound production is called *stridulation* and resembles the way music is produced by drawing a violin bow across the strings. Insects that use this means of making sounds are thus instrumentalists. This technique is common in crickets, grasshoppers, and katydids. Stridulating organs are also found in some cockroaches.

In most cases it is only the males that have "voices." Just why these insects produce sounds is not always clear. In most cases the sounds they make apparently serve to attract the opposite sex; in other cases they are apparently used as a means of communicating danger, or in recognition. On the other hand, it is possible that some insects sing as a warning for others to stay away from their chosen territories. In this respect their songs resemble those of birds.

There are, however, at least two other sound-producing methods employed by insects, but these are not usually found among orthopterans. One is by making buzzing or humming sounds with the wings. We are all familiar with the "angry" buzzing of bees and the hum of the mosquito. Yet another method is by tapping some part of the body against some object. Soldier termites make clicking sounds by tapping their large jaws against the floors of the passages in wood where they live. A few beetles also use this method.

As might be expected in creatures that produce sounds, they also have hearing organs. These organs consist of a membrane or *tympanum* and associated sensory elements. Sound waves

128

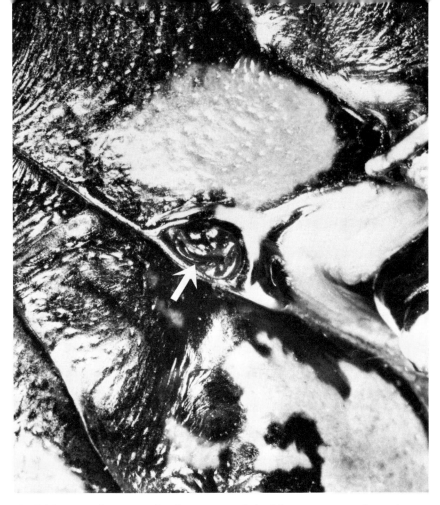

The lubber grasshopper makes hissing sounds by blowing air out of an air pore or spiracle (arrow) on the side of its thorax.

cause the tympanum to vibrate and the sensory organs are stimulated. These "ears" are located on the body or the legs, but never on the head. In the case of long-horned grasshoppers, katydids, and crickets, they are located on the front tibias (leg segments). In the short-horned grasshoppers they are found on the sides of the first segment of the abdomen below the wings. The range of sensitivity of orthopterans is very wide. Crickets hear, or respond, to sound waves from 600 c.p.s. (cycles per second) up to 16,3000 c.p.s. Some long-horned grasshoppers have an even wider range, that is, from 1,600 c.p.s. to 90,000

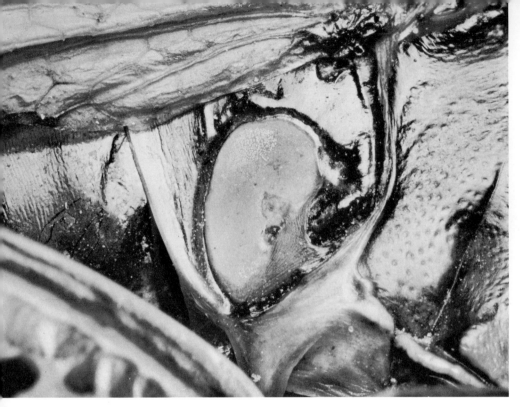

Most grasshoppers' ears or hearing organs are located just below the bases of the wings.

This close-up shows a katydid's hearing organ located on its front leg. The long-horned grasshoppers all have their hearing organs at this point.

c.p.s. The upper limit for man is 20,000 c.p.s. Thus, the long-horned grasshopper can hear far more shrill sounds than can man. Grasshoppers, it has been found, can still detect sounds after their ears have been destroyed. In some kinds the males and females signal to each other by drumming with their feet. In these instances the female is attracted by the song of the male and when she reaches the plant upon which he rests, communication is then carried on by trembling motions transmitted through the plant and felt rather than heard.

The study of insects' songs and sounds is highly complex and requires the use of special electronic equipment.

THE SHORT-HORNED GRASSHOPPERS

Most of these grasshoppers are voiceless, but there are a few exceptions. One of these is the common Carolina locust (*Dissosteira carolina*) that makes a loud crackling sound when in flight. This results from the rubbing of the margins of the hind wings against thickened veins on the fore wings. Just what value this may have to the grasshopper is unknown. This grasshopper's Old World relative, the desert locust, makes a low, clattering noise while in flight. This, it is believed, is caused by the hind wings striking the hind legs.

Another sound-making method used by these grasshoppers is found in several kinds. On the inner surface of each hind femora (largest segment of the hind leg) there is a row of about eighty small peglike teeth. There is also a thickened vein near the base of the front wing. When ready to stridulate, the grasshopper raises both hind legs and rasps them against the raised veins on the surface of each front wing. The wing themselves act as sounding boards. About ninety pulses per second are emitted. One of the most common grasshoppers equipped with this type of sound-making apparatus is *Stenobothrus*.

Perhaps as an indication of grasshopper intelligence, it has been discovered that certain grasshoppers may learn to imitate the songs of other kinds. This occurs when these grasshoppers are placed together in cages. This fact was first noticed by Charles Darwin but, strangely, he attached little importance to it at the time.

The more insects of various kinds are studied, the more are the remarkable facts that come to light. For example, Dr. Richard D. Alexander of the University of Michigan has recently found that a Midwest grasshopper (Paratylotropidia brunneri) communicates by snapping its jaws. This ticking sound may be heard for some distance and is made at the rate of six or seven ticks per second. Dr. Alexander was not only able to tape-record the sound but was successful in obtaining a response from one of the insects by tapping a metal object. These sounds, it was discovered, are produced by both males and females when they are disturbed, and by males when they encounter other males during courtship.

THE LONG-HORNED GRASSHOPPERS AND KATYDIDS

The musical instruments of these insects are located on the wings and consist of a series of notches, the file (located near the base of the left front wing), and of a scraper on the opposite front wing. When in the act of singing or stridulating, the wings are partially raised and sawed back and forth across each other. By this action the scraper rubs across the file, causing the wings to vibrate. This vibration is communicated to the surrounding air by the wings, which act as sounding boards.

By human standards, the songs of these insects are not music. However, they are pleasant sounds of the summer night and evidences of tranquility and peace. The songs of crickets are, in

This close-up shows the singing organs of a katydid. At the base of the left wing is the file and a scraper is on the base of the right wing. When singing, the scraper is rubbed back and forth rapidly across the teeth of the file. The clear areas act like drumheads, communicating the vibrations to the air.

truth, considerably advanced beyond those of katydids; in terms of tonality, cricket songs resemble our own music. Katydids, by contrast, merely saw out rasping noise. If you listen carefully to the song of a katydid you will soon realize that it is not a continuous, rasping sound but one that is interrupted at short intervals by periods of silence. This results from the fact that the scraper is brought into contact with the outer end of the file when the wings are spread apart. The wings are then rapidly closed or brought together, the scraper rubbing swiftly across

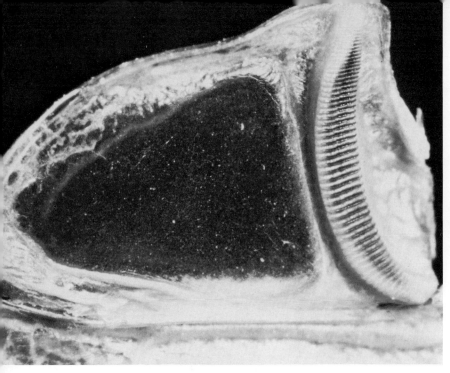

This close-up of the base of a katydid's left wing shows the drum-head and the file.

the teeth of the file. This makes one burst of sound, followed by a period of silence during which the wings are being opened again in preparation for the next burst. This is apparently the general rule. However, there are cases when continuous sound is emitted by the scraper rasping across the file in both directions. The characteristic sounds of various long-horned grasshoppers, katydids, and others result from differences in the number of teeth in the file and in the speed with which the scraper is moved across it. However, the resonant characteristics of the wings, acting as sounding boards, also influence the sounds made by the insects. The number of vibrations per second is designated as cycles per second (c.p.s.) and this determines the *pitch*. There is considerable variation in the pitch in various insect sounds; the true katydid's song (*Pterophylla camellifolia*) is made up of 63,000 c.p.s., while the meadow katydid (*Orchelimum*) emits songs varying in pitch from 7,000 to 27,000 c.p.s. In the cone-headed meadow grasshopper *(Cono-cephalus)*, two sounds are emitted, one at 16,300 c.p.s. and another at 40,000 c.p.s. Few long-horned grasshopers emit sounds lower than about 5,000 c.p.s. but some go as high as 100,000 c.p.s. It is of interest, too, that while the frequency range varies from individual to individual, the *pulse* rate—the intervals between bursts of sound—are fairly constant for each species. This ranges from about three to fifty per second. It may help us to understand how a katydid, for example, makes its sound if we compare it to the way a violin is played. Usually, the bow is drawn back and forth across the strings, sound being produced when the bow is moving in each direction. In the case of the katydid, the "bow" (scraper) is stroked across the "string" (file)

This photograph of a katydid shows the file (upper arrow) at the base of the left wing. The lower arrow points to the ear on the front leg.

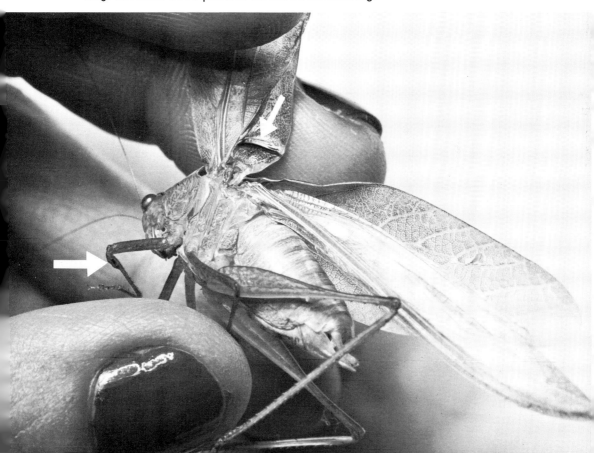

in only one direction and there is a short interval between strokes. This, as we have seen, is the pulse rate. We might also call this the insect's chirp rate.

In addition, the wings of some of these insects are moved so rapidly that their song sounds like a continuous buzz, interrupted at definite intervals by periods of silence. In other words, our ears are not sensitive enough to detect the short time required for the scraper to be brought into position for the next movement across the file and so we hear only a constant buzzing or rasping sound. At definite intervals the insect pauses, then continues its song. This results in pulses. One of the long-horns that uses this system is the large cone-headed katydid (*Neoconocephalus exiliscanorus*) whose song sounds like *dzeet—dzeet—dzeet*. Each *dzeet* is produced by several strokes of the scraper across the file, but it is done so rapidly that to the human ear it appears to be a continuous burst of sound. On the other hand, the large angular-winged katydid (*Microcentrum rhombifolium*) moves its wings very slowly so that the individual clicks made by the scraper on the teeth of the file can be distinctly heard. In this case there are only from 30 to 40 clicks per second.

An interesting feature of many of these insects, as well as of some crickets, is the synchronization of the songs of several individuals. In other words, if one insect is in the act of singing, others that join in apparently have the habit of bringing their notes into the same time rate. One of the best examples is the cone-headed katydid mentioned above. If one of these katydids is producing its usual series of 18 to 25 notes, it will pause now and then and join the chorus of other cone-heads. Its notes are usually timed to synchronize with the rest. In other words, they try "to keep step" with each other. A similar type of singing behavior is found in some birds.

Just as humans from various sections of the country have dis-

A cone-headed katydid (*Neoconocephalus*) saws its front wings back and forth, making a loud rasping sound.

tinctive manners of speech or vernacular expressions, so do many katydids from different areas exhibit variations in their songs. This has been found in at least two katydids, the true katydid (*P. camellifolia*) and the oblong-winged katydid (*Amblycorypha oblongifolia*). These variations in song have probably been evolved over a long period of time by groups of the insects more or less isolated from each other.

The songs of katydids, crickets, and grasshoppers sound different to different people. Thus, they are very difficult to describe. However, it may be of interest to list some of the songs

137

of common long-horns, realizing that they may not sound the same to your ears.

Meadow katydid *(Orchelimum minor)*: *s-s-s-s—s-s-s-s-* or *tsip-tsip-tsip-tsip-tseeeeee*
Cone-headed katydid *(Neoconocephalus)*: *dzeet—dzeet—dzeet—dzeet*
Angular-winged katydid *(Microcentrum rhombifolium)*: *click-click-click-click*
Oblong-winged katydid *(Amblycorypha oblongifolia)*: *it-z-zic——it-z-zic——it-z-zic*
True katydid *(Pterophylla camellifolia)*: *katy-did—she-didn't—she-did* (There are many interpretations)

THE CRICKETS

The sound-making mechanisms of the crickets are quite similar to those of the long-horned grasshoppers and katydids, consisting of a file on one wing and a scraper on the other. In general, what was said regarding their singing techniques is true of the crickets as well. However, the sounds of crickets are quite distinctive and easily recognized. The songs of some common kinds are as follows:

Black field cricket *(Gryllus assimilis)*: *treat-treat-treat*, or *chee-chee-chee*, or *cree-cree-cree-cree*, or (at low-temperatures) *gru-gru-gru*
Tree cricket *(Oecanthus)*: *churr-churr-churr-churr*
Mole cricket *(Gryllotalpa)*: *grr——grr——grr* (deep toned)

Insects are cold-blooded animals and, as such, are strongly influenced by temperature. Thus, the songs of all orthopterans

138

The green snowy tree cricket (*Oecanthus*) is a common singing cricket. Sometimes it is called the "temperature" cricket because, like all crickets and katydids, it sings faster in warm weather, and the temperature can be calculated from its song.

sound different as temperatures vary. Probably the most remarkable case is that of the snowy tree cricket *(Oecanthus)*. Sometimes these delicate little green crickets are also called "temperature crickets." Long ago it was noticed that the chirp rates of these insects were related to prevailing temperatures. It was, in fact, discovered that the temperature could be calculated quite accurately by listening to the song of one of these crickets. This can be done in several ways. One is by counting the number of chirps in 15 seconds and adding 40. This gives the temperature in degrees Fahrenheit. There is only one thing that must be kept in mind; these crickets do not usually sing below 55°F. or above 100°F.

If you prefer, you may determine temperature by the following tables:

Chirps Per Ten Seconds	Temperature (degrees F.)
Black Field Cricket	
5	47
10	54
15	61
20	68
25	75
30	82
35	88
40	96
Snowy Tree Cricket	
5	42
10	55
15	63
20	70
25	77
30	85
35	92
40	100

The songs of the grasshopper and cricket clan have been studied and analyzed in various ways on complex electronic devices and recorded on special equipment. But regardless of the exact ways they sing and the technical details of their songs, their concerts often remain in our memories as pleasant reminders of summer evenings in wild or wooded places.

FOR FURTHER READING

For those who are interested in delving further into the study of grasshoppers and related insects, the following references will be helpful:

GENERAL INFORMATION ON ORTHOPTERA

Blatchley, W. S. *Orthoptera of Northeastern America.* Indianapolis: Nature Publishing Company, 1920.

Frost, S. W. *General Entomology.* New York: McGraw-Hill Book Company, 1942.

Hutchins, Ross E. *Insects.* Englewood Cliffs, New Jersey: Prentice-Hall, Inc., 1966.

Uvarov, B. P. *Locusts and Grasshoppers.* London: Bureau of Imperial Entomology, 1928.

Wigglesworth, V. B. *The Life of Insects.* Cleveland, Ohio: World Publishing Company, 1964.

SONGS OF GRASSHOPPERS AND CRICKETS

Haskell, P. T. *Insect Sounds.* Chicago: Quadrangle Books, 1961.

CAVE-INHABITING CRICKETS

Bailey, Vernon. *Animal Life of Carlsbad Caverns.* Baltimore: The Williams & Wilkins Company, 1928.

———. *Cave Life of Kentucky.* Notre Dame, Indiana: The University Press, 1933.

MIGRATORY HABITS

Gurney, Ashley B. *Grasshopper Glacier.* Washington, D.C.: Annual Report of the Smithsonian Institution, 1952.

Parker, J. R., Newton, R. C., and Shotwell, R. L. *Observations of Mass Flights and Other Activities of the Migratory Grasshopper.* U. S. Department of Agriculture Technical Bulletin No. 1109, 1955.

Wakeland, Claude. *The High Plains Grasshopper.* U. S. Department of Agriculture Technical Bulletin No. 1167, 1958.

———. *Mormon Crickets of North America.* U. S. Department of Agriculture Technical Bulletin No. 1202, 1959.

INDEX

Page numbers in **boldface** *are those on which illustrations appear*

144